D1104152

Quotes

FROM THE EDGE OF NOWHERE

The Art of Noticing Unnoticed Life Wisdoms

Gary Lewis LeRoy, MD

DORRANCE
PUBLISHING CO
EST. 1920
PITTSBURGH, PENNSYLVANIA 15238

Dorrance Publishing Co
585 Alpha Drive
Suite 103
Pittsburgh, PA 15238
Visit our website at *www.dorrancebookstore.com*

ISBN: 978-1-6480-4299-7
eISBN: 978-1-6480-4892-0

AND "I" QUOTE

Preface:

"Another year in my life has come and gone." I suspect you have heard that little voice in your head say something similar on a special occasion like a birthday, anniversary, or a holiday celebration. In my case, the occasion was New Year's Day. After the festivities of the evening had become a blurred, but delightful memory, I reflected on the numerous times I had heard friends and family talk about their lofty resolutions for the coming year. When asked, my traditional response is simply to say, "My resolution is to just be a better human being than I was the previous year." My friends and family can quote me each year, because they know what I will say before I even say it.

However, this year, as I uttered my usual quote, I paused to think more deeply about what I had been regurgitating as a cavalier response each year. During this relatively short journey called "life" there are those among us whose goal it is to improve not only their personal well-being, but also have an innate desire to improve the status of what we often refer to as the human condition of our existence here on Earth. Some of us accomplish this by creating great works of art, life-altering inventions, amazing musical compositions, or architectural marvels. Others champion worthwhile social causes; discover the answer to puzzling scientific mysteries; or simply are great parents, friends, and neighbors. I doubt, however, that each of these great accomplishments had their genesis because the individual just woke up one eventful morning and said, "Today I am going to be a better person than I was yesterday."

My unscientific observation is that most, if not all, great accomplishments occur through a sequence of uniquely random life experiences. Like the genetic protein sequenced life-building blocks of deoxyribonucleic acid (DNA), these sequences of preexisting experiences become linked with a shower of life opportunities that we are exposed to on a daily basis. Remember those five basic senses they taught in grade school? Working in concert, these biological sensory input receptors allow us to **see, touch, smell, hear, taste**, and thus experience our surrounding physical environment. Each moment of the day, we collect critical information to provide us an opportunity to improve or possibly worsen our human conditions based on how we respond or appropriately fail to heed the sensory input provided. Many of us seek a more pleasant life existence by faithfully following socially prescribed conduct or tested algorithms to improve our status. Regardless of our intuitive or deductive reasoning, authorities inform us from childhood that if you follow a certain sequence of social rules of conduct, you will always achieve what you desire. We seek the rules of social wisdom by listening to those we presume to be wise.

How many times have you been present at an event, such as a graduation, conference, political rally, or self-help seminar, when the speaker begins to make a major point by sharing a quote from a recognized social celebrity or dignitary? I have been to hundreds of these events, and they usually say something like, "Let me begin my talk today by sharing a thought with you from [fill in the blank], **and I quote**…" Following, by intent, is a very thought-provoking quote. Thereafter, the speaker begins to weave the subject of his or her lecture around the context of the quote in an effort to engage the listener further.

When you hear one of these quotes, have you ever asked yourself for what reason did the quoted individual speak those words? What was the circumstantial context that caused the person to voice such a quotable quote? In other words, what were they doing, thinking, or experiencing at the time? Did the person attributed with making the historical quote actually author it? Was the quote the brainchild of a talented speechwriter who is destined to remain unknown to the generations of people hearing or reading the immortal words?

On this particular New Year's Day, I found myself thinking of a collection of short quotes I had written down on scraps of paper over the years. These quotes seemed to creep unexpectedly into my consciousness from out of nowhere. Most were generated by something I observed or experienced during my daily work or while interacting with people in real time. For some unknown reason I began to write down these thoughts in an effort to accurately remember them. I eventually began to refer to these thoughts as "I quote" moments.

I could not attribute these quotes to any orator past or present. I have since used a few of them in speeches, but most of the quotes have been filed away to be included on my list of things to ponder in later life.

For some unknown reason, the mounting number of quotes nagged my spirit more than usual on this particular New Year's Day. I finally yielded to the desire to contemplate the quotes I had collected. I began the journey of taking some of these quotes and sharing them in the form of a book. Unlike the crafting of most books, my experimental design involved selecting ten of my quotes at random (yes, I placed the seventy plus quotes in a cookie jar and randomly selected ten) and a chapter of my book is dedicated to each.

The purpose of this book is to share with the reader my conscious attempt to fulfill my resolution of evolving into a better human through the practical use of the "I quote" wisdom whispered into my subconscious brain. The ethereal force revealing these quotes from the edge of nowhere granted me rare opportunities to sense the constant presence of alternative life directions. Prior to acknowledging the whispers, I had simply elected to listen, write down the message, and just move on doing business as usual.

The fact that you are reading these words indicates that you, too, may be on a journey to improve your status of life well-being. Perhaps you are no longer content with just living life as usual. Maybe you, too, have several "I quote" messages whispering in your unconscious mind — begging to be recognized and acted upon. Something deep inside the darkest crevices of your human spirit challenges you to search for a more joyfully fulfilled life. Your answers may have always been present, but just been outside of your emotional reach. I hope that after reading this book, or even just a few of the chapters with themes that garner your attention, you will begin the process of creating your own life quotes to live by. Use them as your soul's torchlight to see the way more clearly toward life's most genuine treasures.

Contents

"When you awake each morning ask yourself, 'What will I do today to improve the world for someone other than myself?' Because the day will surely come when you will awake no more."

"It is difficult to become the voice of reason in a crowded room when you can't even remember why you are in the room."

"A seed of doubt once planted in a field of obvious truth will grow so rapidly that it obscures reality."

"When we speak about how we feel about an event — this is gossip; when we report on what we think was observed — this is news; when society writes about the residual evidence of the event—this is history. The truth is that only God will ever know the reality of what really happened."

"Destiny and fate will always offer us opportunities to change the status quo."

"The ONLY genuine expert opinion of the future is one given by someone who has been to the future and returned to the present to reveal their personal experience of what tomorrow has in store."

"You have to go past knowledge and truth in the dictionary before you arrive at WISDOM."

"Promise nothing but act as if you have."

"We need to teach our youth to become men and women of great character and how not to simply grow up to be characters."

"Fate has its virtue."

Introduction

Several years ago, my daughters, Julia and Ciara, gave me a birthday gift—an ancient-looking three- by five-inch journal. Inside the soft brown, inch-thick leather-bound journal were lined blank pages with nothing on them except for personal messages on the first pages from each of my daughters. The message from my oldest daughter, Julia, was a reflection on how her "whole mindset" about her life had changed after one year of her college education. She realized that much of what she had learned in college was a reaffirmation of what I had taught her as a concerned parent "…way back when." There were many opportunities for her mother and me to provide our children with what we suspected were valuable life lessons. While raising children, many unexpected and unrehearsed teachable moments arise. It is impossible for parents to verify how much of what we say to our children is heard, ignored, or retained.

Well, apparently, they both retained more than I had anticipated. Nevertheless, despite our early life warnings, they each needed to verify a variety of these parental life lessons on their own through personal experience. This is a natural part of growing up. How many of us were warned not to touch the hot stove, but when the grown-ups were not looking, touched it anyway—or at least came very close—to verify that it really would burn our tiny fingers? Julia wrote, "So, I guess what I'm trying to say is, thank you for always being there to give me good advice and to bail me out when I didn't follow that advice. Thank you for letting me grow up and learn those valuable lessons on my own."

Julia went on to explain why she and Ciara decided to give me the gift of the little brown journal. They wanted to provide me with a gift that was, "Completely and totally for and about you." It was a gift given out of love. Its intention was to give me a blank space to write down my thoughts; my frustrations; my inner most secrets; or even just random thoughts arriving out of nowhere during the course of the day. Julia felt it was an important tool for me to use so I could stop for a moment, jot down my thoughts, and clear my head of my soul's subconscious background noise muffling my ability to function effectively during a busy day.

That little brown journal sat on my desk for years. Both daughters are now college graduates. But I did take their advice and began writing down my random thoughts in the form of "thought quotes," or what I like to refer to as my "I quotes," that spring out of nowhere to populate my consciousness with thought-provoking wisdom.

Too many of you have sat through mandatory meetings sponsored by your employer, a non-profit organization, religious affiliated group, school, or alumni association. You name it; you have sat through it. The charge of meeting attendees is to create a mission and/or vision statement. The intent of the mission statement is the adoption of common language used when explaining to others **why** the organization exists and **why** it is relevant to the current social environment. As I sit through these exercises, it always amazes me that many of these organizations have existed for years, if not decades, but had never asked themselves two essential questions: 1) "Why do we need to exist?" 2) "Is what we did in the past still relevant today?"

While many organizations have a mission statement plastered on a wall or filed away in an obscure gray metal filing cabinet, shocking numbers of employees and volunteers have no clue about the true measures of their organization's success or failure. When the gravity of failure is already pulling an organization toward extinction, initiating a mission-statement seminar to maintain market share, improve consumer confidence, increase membership, bolster contributions, create public relevance, or prevent impending demise is inadvisable.

Now, let us take this concept of mission statements to a personal level. Writing a life mission statement is one of many tools used by counselors, psychologists, psychiatrists, and self-help seminar gurus. Employers and organizations ask their employees and volunteers to assist them in creating mission-statement language to best define **why** the organization is relevant. Yet many of those asked to participate in this exercise are personally struggling to understand how to find joy or enduring relevance in their own lives. Before attempting to save others, make certain you first know the instructions on how to save yourself.

The underlying message I received from my daughters through the gift of the little brown journal was that they both recognized an essential need for me to save myself. I needed to take a moment to hit life's pause button. It was great advice that I urge you to consider. Begin to practice by turning off the television; put away the cell phone; tear up the to-do list. If you can do this for just thirty minutes a day, it will be a good start on the road toward finding inward joy.

During this brief pause, create at least one "I quote" to get you through the day, the month, or the year. Your quote can be a temporary mission statement to lighten an emotional burden, or a torchlight statement that guides you away from the darkest crevices of failure. The important message here is that you internalize the quote(s). Print it on a T-shirt; use it as a screensaver on your computer or phone; put it on a poster; or even imprint it on a message posted on your doorway so you can see it as you leave home each day.

I do not intentionally sit down and think up quotes. They come to me both during the quiet pauses and during the noise of the day. Every quote introduced in this book seemed to stumble into me from out of nowhere. Each quote found me as I was experiencing the routine of my day-to-day, ho-hum life. I would encourage you to allow quotes to find you as you experience life. When your quote finds you, hit the pause button and write it down. Afterward, take a brief moment to reflect about the reason this life mission quote spoke to you.

I have over seventy of these "I quotes" [they are entitled "I" quotes because they are "my" quotes] that found me over the past twenty-plus years. What follows are the first ten quotes I randomly selected to share with you by typing each quote on a scrap of paper and placing them all in my kitchen cookie jar. I drew them from the jar one at a time. I wrote the chapters of this book in the sequence I drew the quotes from the cookie jar. You might think that this is a foolish way to compose a book, but I am a firm believer that life is not always a random sequence of asynchronous events.… "Fate has its virtue." Read the chapters in any sequence your spirit tells you to do so.

CHAPTER ONE

"When you awake each morning ask yourself, 'What will I do
today to improve the world for someone other than myself?'
Because the day will surely come when you will awake no more."

nce upon a time... when we were children, there were no boundaries to our imagination or the possibilities of what we wanted to become when we grew into adulthood. Our choices were endless, and usually based on what we learned or experienced from interacting with our parents, relatives, or friends. Sometimes the possibilities emerged from what we learned about the world around us, from our experiences at school, or from the books we read. Today, social media (i.e. internet access sites, cell phone apps, radio, television, etc.) exposes children to an even wider universe of possibilities.

A child's idea about what they want to become in life evolves from fantasies of becoming a Power Ranger who saves the galaxy from super villains to something more realistic, like being a firefighter who saves potential victims from raging flames. At one point in my youth, I wanted to be an astronaut. My interest in the National Aeronautical and Space Administration's (NASA) efforts in the 1960s to fulfill President John F. Kennedy's vision of sending a man to the moon by the end of the decade, in large part, fueled this ambition.

I read everything I could get my hands on regarding the science of astronomy and space exploration. I devoured newspaper articles about advances made by NASA, especially with regard to the Apollo moon shot missions. Night after night, I sat in the cool grass of my backyard staring at the moon, wondering why the grand object never fell to earth. I recall watching the little black and white TV in our kitchen on the very early morning of July 20, 1969 as Neil A. Armstrong exited the lunar module *Eagle* to become the first human to step on that object that had occupied so many hours of my attention. Like the astronauts, I, too, wanted to defy gravity. I had a burning desire someday — like a starship captain — to boldly journey where no one had ever gone before.

Like many boys my age, I read a lot of comic books. As a result, somehow I wanted to develop super powers like my favorite characters. In hopes of unleashing a yet unrevealed ability to lift one-ton boulders, run at super speed, or defy the laws of gravity as I flew above the clouds without wings, I exercised diligently. Sitting in my room, I stared at the wall hoping that by some miracle, my gift of x-ray vision would suddenly kick in and reveal the contents of the room on the other side. Most of all, I wanted to become a superhero who used superhuman gifts to save lives by helping those in need.

Despite my best efforts, I finally conceded the fact that I had not been blessed with any noticeable superhuman powers. I recognized that my career as a superhero was probably not going to become a reality. At age twelve, I seriously began considering alternative professional development options. One evening after my mother had gotten off work, I went to her room to have a very deep discussion about how I could make the world a better place — absent the use of any special powers to assist me. "What do I need to do to improve the world for someone other than myself?" I asked her.

As the only child in my household, I had the opportunity to indulge my mother in many uninterrupted, probing conversations. It was common for me to end my day sitting on my mother's bedroom floor doing homework while also chattering with her about what I had done in school during the day. During one very memorable conversation, I recall getting up off the floor and bouncing up her bed to ask her if, when she was my age, she was ever bothered by all the bad things that were happening in the world around her. I wanted to know what I could do to help others live a better life. That evening she instilled in my heart the value of an education and the importance of placing the needs of those we serve before our own personal desires. From that moment, I began to sense a certain degree of unexplainable urgency in my life.

Up to this point in my young life, few things qualified as earning the status of urgent. I was barely teetering on the edge of adolescence, so why had this random conversation ignited such a pondering of the future in my spirit?

Much later in life, I would learn the science of how haphazard genetic malformations can fatally disrupt a human embryo's delicate development process in nearly half of all early pregnancies. These genetic hiccups can result in a life-altering birth defect, preterm labor, or fetal demise — vanquishing the opportunity for a new life to be born into the world. Our presence in the stream of human existence is nothing short of a miracle.

However, if the fetus wins the genetic chess match of reproduction, a more sinister game of chance awaits them at birth. Even those babies fortunate enough to be born with an otherwise healthy biological blueprint must directly contend with external environmental challenges. Each day thousands of babies are born into the presence of suboptimal environmental conditions: war-ravaged countries, communities plagued with disease, dysfunctional family situations, or desperately impoverished social environments. Despite these biological and environmental obstacles, the majority of our youth survive to take on the ambiguities of adolescent self-discovery. This phase of life is not immune to social status or economic privilege. Enduring the sting of lost love, missed opportunity, social misadventures, emerging sexuality, body image, and an innate desire to understand an unexplainable world around them becomes a psychological minefield during these formative years. Many emerge from their childhood or adolescence with invisible, yet permanent, emotional damage that never entirely heals throughout their adulthood.

One of my freshman high school teachers once told me, "You think very old for your young age." I have heard this described as a young person having an old soul. At the time she said this to me I accepted it as an unsolicited compliment, but I was uncertain why she shared this with me. She must have sensed the urgency I was feeling about my life direction. Far ahead of my early teenage existence, I could already envision the invading reality awaiting me as the specter of age would relieve me of youthful physical trappings.

At some point in my life, I would also relinquish my youthful delusion of immortality. Even as a teenager, I had already begun to wander through life with much more care as I suddenly recognized my expiration date could prematurely arrive—as had unfortunately happened to several of my childhood friends through illness, accidents, or senseless social violence. Vitality wanes; accidents, medical disorders, and disease cripple our bodies; or unescapable emotional and/or physical deterioration incapacitate us. Somehow, at a very young age, I could already see this path of life waiting to challenge me. This urgent primordial instinct pushed me emotionally to appreciate the immeasurable blessing of each day of life. My "old" thoughts had revealed a treasure some people take a lifetime to discover.

So even as a child, I had already begun to feel an urgency to improve the world for someone other than myself. Perhaps this urgent flame to serve others ignited after the conversation I had with my mother on that late summer evening. Perhaps it was always there, resting in my consciousness simply awaiting the appropriate moment to be kindled.

As I sat at my cluttered desk pondering this chapter, I desperately attempted to remember the exact time, location, and circumstance when the quote initially crept into my consciousness. The answer is not certain to me. For whatever reason, I never developed the habit of placing dates on the quotes. I simply wrote them down and put them away for future reference. Sometimes the quotes spontaneously awakened me from a nocturnal slumber—like a spiritual muscle cramp. They often pester me until I get out of bed and relieve myself by depositing the words onto a piece of paper. Many others arrive in the daylight while I am alone in the car driving, walking on a quiet trail, or soaking in a warm tub of water and suds. Silence is not always the protagonist for the arrival of these quotes. They can approach me in a crowded room alive with fusing blends of voices echoing from ceiling to floor. The quote arrives effectively silencing the noises surrounding my spirit by transporting my thoughts to the edge of nowhere — where the quote can best be overheard.

"When you awake, each morning ask yourself, 'What will I do today to improve the world for someone other than myself?' Because the day will surely come when you will awake no more."

Another quote came to me years after this one, but was not one of the ten I pulled from the cookie jar at random. It said, "I long to be the best person I have ever known." I suspect this quote emerged from the substrate of the other. I now find myself awaking each day realizing, now more than ever, given the timeline of human life expectancy, my expiration date is rapidly approaching. Thus, I ask myself in a conscious prayer, "What can I do today to improve the life of someone other than myself?"

Each of us has an undetermined expiration date when our existence among the living will end. During our timeline, the following sequence of events occurs in some fashion. Based on their life experiences, our parents or guardians teach us how effectively to **live** in a social environment. We **learn** from our human experiences to expect certain outcomes when we interact with others in our society. We encounter genuine **love** or affections for specific human beings; and at some point, many of us feel an urgency to leave a **legacy** we hope will live on beyond our human existence.

As we travel though life, it is much easier to focus our attention on the one person we know the best — the person you see staring at you in the mirror every day. Of course, it is instinctive for us to take care of our biological needs (providing ourselves with food, water, and shelter from the elements). This is followed closely by our need to provide for and protect those people (i.e. spouse, children, biological relatives, social acquaintances, you get the picture) we have chosen to love or who have demonstrated an enduring love for us. As we learn about the social order we are randomly born into, our focus expands to include friends and acquaintances who have shared experiences and expectations regarding religious doctrine, socioeconomic customs, ethnic traditions, or geopolitical values. This creates what we often refer to as our established "cultural norm." With twenty-first-century technologies, our circle of social awareness can now expand to the most remote corners of the earth. This provides each of us with infinite opportunities never previously possible in human existence. If we desire, we can **live** among, **learn** from, **love**, and leave a **legacy** for populations of people on the planet who we would not have known existed if we lived our lives 100 years prior. As strange as it may seem, sometimes these unknown populations of people do not live on the other side of the planet — they may live within walking distance of us. Many of the people we need to discover exist in our own city, in the building where we work, or are within our own neighborhood. We simply need to recognize their presence.

It is easier to think about self and the tight cultural bubble surrounding us; but it is far more spiritually fulfilling to improve that portion of the world existing outside of our familiar acquaintances. If each of us dedicated just a portion of our day to doing one random unselfish act of kindness for someone who does not exist within our cultural norm — be it locally or globally — eventually our seemingly small acts of consistent kindness will return magnified as a legacy destined to live beyond the day we awake no more.

⊹⊱┄┄┄┄⊰⊹

… Live now with all the vitality you can offer. Learn all that you can about the world surrounding you. Now is the time to tell all those you care deeply about that you love them. These are the urgent and essential aspects of a life well lived.

CHAPTER TWO

"It is difficult to become the voice of reason in a crowded room when you can't even remember why you are in the room."

$\mathcal{H}$ave you ever been invited to an event or meeting and not felt genuinely engaged with any of individuals in the room? I think most of us have been there and experienced the emotional discomfort associated with this situation. Worse yet, have you ever provided what you thought was a good idea early during a conversation only to have it ignored; but when mentioned later in the discussion by another participant, the majority of the people in the room thought it was a stroke of genius? At that point, you began to wonder what value your presence brings to the gathering. You are perplexed as to why no one heard what you initially proposed and why now, when proposed by someone else, the idea is brilliant. If they were not listening to the voice of reason [you] earlier in the conversation, who were they listening to?

I often go to meetings with certain preconceived notions regarding likely accomplishments based on my review of the program or agenda. However, once I have comfortably situated myself in my chosen seat, I begin to scan the faces of those in attendance. I wonder how many people are there, only for acknowledgment in the meeting minutes. They aren't mentally present. Yes, that's right. I said it. On many occasions, I have even been one of those individuals who drag my baggage of distracting random thoughts into the meeting room with me. I acknowledge that this preexisting baggage of mental distractions blunt my ability to be fully present in the conversation.

With that said, let's begin by doing some psychosocial science homework. Make the following observations the next time you go out to a restaurant or attend your next business meeting. At the restaurant look for a table with a group of four or more people. Be careful not to stare too long—that would just be creepy—but observe how many of the people at the table are actively engaged in conversation. If someone is not participating in the conversation, what are they doing? Oddly enough I have observed situations like this where everyone at the table was more involved in interacting with their cell phone than with the people at the table. Most often I observe at least one individual who seems to be deep in thought about something unrelated to the others dining at the table. They seem to have a certain "far away" look in their eyes telegraphing the fact that only their physical body is sitting there at the table. Their mental spirit has swept them to the edge of elsewhere. I ponder to myself if anyone at this person's table is aware of the lonesome individual's emotional absence.

At certain meetings, I look around the table to see how many of those present are consistently maintaining eye contact and responding with affirming nonverbal body language to the individual(s) speaking. How many are checking email on their cell phone, surfing the web on their laptop, sorting through paperwork, doodling on the agenda, checking the insides of their eyelids for cracks (sleeping), or are obviously far away in thought unrelated to the meeting? We have all been there. If there was a sign at the meeting room door instructing all who enter to, **"leave your nonessential outside thoughts at the door as you enter"** how many of us would be capable of doing so?

This marvelous thing we call the human mind is only capable of completely focusing on one task at a time. However, the body's central control station — the brain — is also capable of controlling millions of delicately balanced essential autonomic biophysical functions of the human body beneath our awareness. These essential functions consistently keep us connected with the world around us. These **executive functions** are housed in what I refer to as the "up front and personal" control center of the human brain — the **prefrontal cortex**. This decision-making portion of our brain is where our life planning and goal setting functions occur. Essential impulse-inhibiting safeguards — our social police officer — are also housed in the prefrontal cortex. In contrast, to the slower processing prefrontal control center are the rapid first-responder centers of the brain called the **amygdala and limbic structures**. These species survival fail-safe structures are housed deep in the brain for rapid reaction to external fight or flight motivations. Frustration, fear, anger, threats, terrors, and sexual arousal are rudimentary biological accelerants capable of igniting these areas of the brain.

This delicate process becomes unbalanced when confronted with an enormity of spiritual or emotional distractions.

These disruptions to our ever-present sentinels in the amygdala and limbic structures release subliminal doses of stress neurotransmitters to engage the body in a biophysical civil war within seconds. The collateral damage of this internal war results in a loss of our ability to effectively concentrate [memory lapses]; appropriately digest our food [digestive disorders]; feel energized [chronic fatigue]; experience rejuvenating sleep patterns [insomnia/sleep disorders]; prevent emotional burnout [anxiety disorders]; or experience genuine happiness [major depression].

It is virtually impossible to completely detach ourselves from our emotional brain and leave what is contained in our thoughts outside the door if besieged by a war of concealed emotions going on just beneath the surface. These distractions keep us from being the voice of reason in a crowded room when we feel hopeless, unwanted, unloved, or unworthy of being present. The result is we become one of the wandering corporate zombies who show up in the "C" suite but are never truly present.

"It is difficult to become the voice of reason in a crowded room when you can't even remember why you are in the room."

I seem to recall this quote falling into my conscious space when I was at a meeting and I was doing my social homework of human observation. One of those standard reoccurring monthly meetings that most of us attend out of obligation, there was no foregone conclusion that something of intrinsic value would result from the discussions. The meeting began several minutes after the designated start time. Several people with disinterested expressions on their faces straggled in several minutes after the meeting began. As we lumbered through the agenda, I looked around to see who was paying attention. I knew that I wasn't. I had genuinely tuned out about fifteen minutes into my people-watching portion of the program. There was an element of quiet disengagement filtering through the room. Attendees were busy checking cell phones beneath the table. Heads bobbed as people forcefully snapped their necks to an upright position to prevent gravity from overtaking their cranial weight thus sending their faces crashing onto the table. During my observations, I reengaged to inject what I thought was a reasonable and pertinent strategic suggestion, but at some point during my comments it became obvious that the presenter was patiently waiting for my mouth to stop moving so his rebuttal could begin. Spoiler alert: I realized not only the agenda, but the meeting outcome had been pre-planned. Our job was to hear the message, "buy in" to the preconceived plan, and accept the inevitable.

This was the catalyst for the culture of quiet disengagement I observed fueling the mood in the room. Unlike myself, most of the veterans of these meetings knew the protocol of physically showing up and being counted as present. They had long since resigned the effort of bringing any emotional energy to these gatherings. If pressed, most in attendance probably could not effectively summarize the highlights of the meeting an hour afterwards, other than to state, "It was a meeting about 'X,' and I was required to attend." Attendees had no idea why their mental presence was required in the room, so it was elsewhere.

This "C" suite situation can also happen at home with those individuals who we profess to love. Our sense of chronic disengagement provides subliminal evidence that loved ones are unworthy of our full attention. This is the emotional spark capable of igniting a delicate biopsychological civil war beneath the surface of any human being present in the room. When this limited attention happens to a young person, a lifetime of collateral emotional damage can result. Our youth have a limited array of personal life experiences at their disposal to make evidenced-based determinations on how to navigate their social environment logically. While their brain's higher executive cognitive functions are maturing, it is instinctive for our young to pattern their social behaviors after their trusted caretakers. Our human Deoxyribonucleic Acid (DNA) provides each of us with a basic genetic blueprint of what we are capable of becoming.

A child may desire to grow to 6 feet 5 inches tall, but if his/her DNA instructs the body to grow to 5 feet 7 inches tall, the outcome isn't altered by wishing it to be so. However, our human DNA does not imprint us with cultural norms, religious values, or political viewpoints. As we mature into young adulthood, we look toward those who have lived before us to provide the next generation with wise advice on how to use our basic DNA attributes to live a purpose-driven existence. We desire their full attention. The assumption is that they are in our life to guide us through our turbulent years of self-discovery.

At some point in our young life, we desire to have the question, "Why am I here?" answered. Even as we grow beyond young adulthood, we look toward our trusted social elders to grant us knowledge about a life path worthy of following. How many times have you asked an older someone, "Why did you decide to become a [fill in the blank]?" Most respond with a story about a special someone who inspired them during their formative years. At a critical juncture in our existence, someone was the torchbearer who set the neurotransmitters in our brain ablaze. This resulted in a dampening of the toxic neurological receptors of fear capable of impeding our path toward a courageous new life adventure, choosing a particular professional career, or selecting a righteous life path to follow. If we marginalize family members, friends, coworkers, or members of society, the opposite is certain to result. They feel unworthy of experiencing the joy of a life well lived. Similar to the young who inquire, those who dwell in the shadowed margins of society demand an answer to the, "Why am I here?" question. It is imperative that we listen to our fellow human beings and acknowledge their presence. We must stand ready to provide others with more than just our physical presence when they thirst for our full attention. If we are incapable or unwilling to honestly answer the "Why am I here" question for those who we live on this planet with, we are effectively contributing to our own social deterioration.

Out of our youthful observations flow boundless dreams of new opportunities never imagined by previous generations. During our somewhat limited appearance in the linage of human existence, we each attempt to master the art of being in complete control of the culture surrounding us. Some of us attempt to control our lives by emulating others who appear to have been successful in manipulating social perceptions.

Many unquestionably admire this illusion of control if it garnishes the individual with tremendous personal fame or fortune during their life journey. Other individuals study selected religious doctrine to provide them with spiritual clarity about how best to experience a joyful life existence. Unfortunately, there are those who elect to dampen their senses with mood modifying agents to alter their perception of the joyless uncertainties of life. The best tool in any inspired individual's personal toolbox is the ability to free themselves from the shackles of biased traditions or cultural norms obscuring evidence of the intrinsic value of the nearly eight billion other human beings temporarily sharing the world with them.

As the years of my life pass, my opinions about a variety of social topics are more strident. I have also grown more acutely aware of the enormity of what I do not know. I sense we have dragged far too many nineteenth- and twentieth-century social biases forward with us into the twenty-first century. The internet, social media and a 24/7 news cycle saturate our lives and, as a result, it is increasingly difficult to filter fact from near-fact or fiction. Our amazing, but primitive, brains have not evolved enough to acclimate to this constant onslaught of sensory-media interference. So many lessons I learned in my youth, and even in my latter days, have proven invalid. I have learned that it is the wisest of humans who knows what he/she does not know. Fact: **Knowledge verified by objective facts is priceless, but random information without truth is worthless.**

As I involve myself with more social outreach programs in my extended community, I reveal my spirit to a more diverse group of inhabitants of the earth. These individuals have their own personal view of the same world on which I am residing. These interactions with people unlike myself sharpen my understanding of the numerous social cultures surrounding me. While I am not obliged to believe in the world, as others perceive it, I have become a better inhabitant of the earth armed with an improved understanding of others' points of view. I have also come to realize the potential liability of bringing real-world experience viewpoints to a discussion with others who have only confirmed their beliefs through "virtual" authorities. An opposing voice of "experientially" confirmed evidence will quickly silence a crowded room in disbelief. One of the many assets of growing older is the ability to tell a young person that what they think is an original idea, is no more original than it was when you thought it thirty years ago. I hated when an older person told me this when I was a teenager, but somehow it feels good sharing it with young people now.

Therefore, I encourage you to have the courage to share your personal life experiences with others. Tell them your story of how persons in your life inspired you by unselfishly giving you their **full attention and devotion**. Resist the temptation to have just an abundance of virtual acquaintances in lieu of seeking enduring **experiential relationships** with a diverse collection of true friends and loving family. The latter will bring fulfillment and an enduring joy.

Always seek wisdom in alphabetical order. First be <u>Aware</u> of your lack of knowledge; <u>Educate</u> yourself to seek knowledge; build on your <u>Knowledge</u> to arrive at the truth; When the <u>Truth</u> is confirmed, then and only then will your journey conclude with a direct path to <u>Wisdom</u>.

CHAPTER THREE

"A seed of doubt once planted in a field of obvious truth will grow so rapidly that it obscures reality."

$\mathcal{I}$ mentioned in the introduction of this book that I selected these ten quotes randomly from my kitchen cookie jar. I wrote each chapter in the order the quotes came out of the jar. So, it was somewhat surprising how this quote followed the previous quote about being the voice of reason in a crowded room.

Before I get into where this quote emerged, indulge me for a few paragraphs while I tell you about my kitchen cookie jar. When I was four years old, my mother and I moved to the only childhood home I can remember. The only reason I know that I was four is because that is the age "Mommy" told me I was when we moved to the little white house on Williams Street with the four large wooden pillars on the front porch. There are certain aspects of our youth we recollect as disconnected glimpses from fading fragmented memories of our childhood. We know that they happened, or at least we think they happened, because they seem so real. This is where we sometimes must depend on someone like a parent or an older sibling to verify that an event from our early childhood actually occurred.

I can now confirm with certainty that the house I grew up in on Williams Street was considerably smaller than the enormous rooming house we resided in for the first four years of my life at 123 North Summit Street in Dayton, Ohio. Mommy and I had lived there with family members who, like my mother, worked as sharecroppers in the cotton fields of Mississippi and migrated up North to find factory jobs with regular work hours and better pay. Other than the four large wooden pillars on the porch, that made it look like the White House in Washington, DC, my only initial memory of our house on Williams Street was the cookie jar sitting on top of the large white Frigidaire refrigerator in the kitchen. I could barely see it from my four-year-old height-restricted point of view, but it was shaped like a large red apple with green leaves that formed the top and handle. I do recall Mommy taking it down off the refrigerator and setting it on the kitchen table. With me bouncing in her lap, she gave me cookies as a reward for good behavior. That was the only time I got a close look at the cookie jar's features. I later realized why it sat on top of the refrigerator. It was to keep the reward out of my reach.

I recall spending what seemed like hours, but it was probably only a few restless minutes, sitting on the light green tiled kitchen floor staring at that apple wondering about the contents. What type of cookies had Mommy put in there? *I hope that they are Oreos*, I thought to myself. I loved Oreos. On particularly boring days, I would stare at the distance between the floor and the cookie jar conjuring up ingenious ways to get that jar off the top of the refrigerator without my mother's knowledge. After many failed attempts, I defaulted to asking myself, *How good do I have to be to get a cookie from the big apple cookie jar?*

Thus, I had a flashback moment when I placed my quotes in the cookie jar that now sets on my refrigerator. I won it at a silent auction charity event. While it is not shaped like an apple, it reminded me of the cookie jar that remains a consistent fixture on the top of the refrigerator at Mommy's house. Mine has images of children from across the world painted around its base and the handle on top is in the shape of a globe. When I pulled the quote for this chapter from out of my cookie jar, I immediately recalled jotting it down years ago, but I had to think to myself, *Where from the edge of nowhere did that come?*

Some things we accept as obvious truths. The sun comes up in the eastern sky each morning and provides us with daylight. The sun sets in the western sky resulting in nighttime. If we drop something, gravity will accelerate it toward the ground. These are just two examples of physical laws we all accept as verifiable truths. We can figure these things out without spending years in school learning about astrophysics and gravitational vector fields. Without the benefit of a formal education, we know them to be facts without a detailed understanding of why they happen. If suddenly the sun were to come up in the southern sky one morning, or if I were to let go of a hammer and it were to fly up instead of falling down, I would immediately think I was dreaming or going insane. My entire expectation of truth would have to adapt to a new reality that is contrary to what is hardwired into my unconscious brain by a lifetime of experiencing certainties about the world around me. The first astronauts had to consciously re-adjust their brain to accept the fact that without Earth's grav-itational pull, when they released an object it would not land on the floor of the spacecraft. Given their constantly changing orbit of the earth, they could no longer use the presence of the sun in space to define accurately what was daytime versus nighttime.

The apple-shaped cookie jar was there on top of the refrig-erator every day of my early childhood. If I did something good, like eat all my green vegetables or go to bed without a fuss, I could ask for a cookie and the jar would consistently find its way to the kitchen table. Although there were not al-ways Oreos in the jar, there were some sort of cookies. That was reality as I knew it.

But what happens to our view of the world when our ex-pectations of social reality are disrupted by a seed of doubt. Uncertainty can sprout from many sources. Remember how our parents would amuse us with fairy tales when we were children? We did not question whether the stories were tales of fact or fiction because as toddlers the only frame of refer-ence available to us was the world as provided by our parent(s) or guardian(s). Once upon a time, our parents knew everything, because everything we didn't know, they knew the answer to—or at least they gave us an answer (factual or not). Infants become curious toddlers who begin to explore more than their environment. They arrive at an age of discov-ery where they begin to constantly ask grown-ups, "Why [fill in the blank]?" Why is the sky blue? Why don't birds fall out the sky? Why is ice cold? Why do people boo-boo? Why do I have to go to sleep? Why do things die? Etcetera, etcetera, etcetera. They trust older human beings to be reliable authorities to provide them with truths about the expanding world they are discovering for the first time.

Sometimes adults intentionally do not provide children with accurate information just to perpetuate whimsical social fantasies or to keep them from unintentional harm. How many of you to this day cannot swallow a solid watermelon seed without thinking that a five-pound green stripped watermelon will suddenly grow in your stomach and require emergency surgery? At least in my house this is what kept me from swallowing watermelon seeds. Guess who told me the unverified "truth" about swallowing watermelon seeds? If this was Mommy's way of preventing me from choking on large watermelon seeds, it proved to be an effective deterrent.

We ended chapter two with acknowledgment that our subconscious alphabetical path of discovery in life begins with **awareness** followed by the pursuit of **education**; then the acquisition of **knowledge**; then verifiable **truth**; and ending in **wisdom**. A subset of awareness is self-awareness. Prior to seeking a path toward wisdom, it is essential for each of us to become self-aware of which truths we are willing to accept as the self-evident realities of living life on Earth. As we mature into more independent self-aware species (young adulthood) we consciously begin our selection of which truths to adhere. Those proven factually inaccurate are either adjusted to fit within an established social or political paradigm or abandoned to be replaced by a verifiable truth. It would seem logical for humans to jettison any proven inaccurate notions when they are making critical life decisions. However, this is not always the case. Many humans are unable to undo the inaccurate experiential hardwiring in their brain despite obvious evidence that it is invalid information. This can create a self-inflicted biased or prejudiced view of the world in which we reside. (Author's note: I am prejudice against certain color watermelon seeds. I still do not swallow those hard-brown watermelon seeds. The little white ones cannot grow in your stomach. That's a fact — I think).

We begin life as a biological organism armed with a genetic blueprint that provides us with predetermined physical characteristics and an array of genetic probabilities manifesting as certain human physiologic attributes and/or certain specific predetermined medical disorders. This genetic blueprint constructed from protein sequences of deoxyribonucleic acid (DNA) provides the superstructure of the human we are **capable** of becoming. The social structure into which we are born provides the psychosocial brick and mortar used to construct the human we **do** become.

Each of us begins life on an instinctive journey of discovery to expand our individual awareness of the world around us. Based on parameters imposed by family values, religious or nonreligious beliefs, education, economic limitations, political beliefs/barriers, or our ability to experience the norms of different cultures, we consciously arrive at an individualized "trusted view" of the world by early adulthood.

Let's look at an example of how an inaccurate trusted view of our world can diminish potential. A child is born being blessed with a strong underlying genetic blueprint consistent with the capacity to become an Olympic decathlon athlete or a fortune 500 chief executive officer. If the child grows up and never becomes aware of these capabilities because their trusted view of their world is shrouded by social obstacles preventing him/her from fully unleashing those capabilities, it is unlikely that an Olympic medal or CEO bonus check will be a reality in their future. We have heard cases of identical twins separated at birth being placed in significantly different social environments. Given disparagingly different social-economic environments, one child may grow up to climb the social ladder of success with ease while their genetically matched twin struggles to hang on to the bottom rung of the societal ladder.

"A seed of doubt once planted in a field of obvious truth will grow so rapidly that it obscures reality."

I spent fourteen years growing up in the little white house on Williams Street in Dayton, Ohio with the four large wooden pillars and the apple cookie jar on the refrigerator. By the time, I could retrieve those cookies from the jar on my own, I had determined my "trusted view" of the world. I had no doubt that I could grow up to do whatever I wished with my life if I only dedicated my mind to focus all my effort to the task. To keep getting those cookies, I stayed within the strict social lines Mommy had drawn. I valued what she valued. I prayed as she prayed. I learned how to work hard and save some money for what my mother classified as, "hard times." Despite being the only little "colored" kid in my neighborhood for a few years,

I never recognized it as a limitation. It just made me unique.

It wasn't until a summer afternoon when I was asked by a neighborhood friend to go to the swimming pool at a local park that the first seed of doubt was planted deeply into my young soul. At that point in my life I had never been to a real public swimming pool. By "real" I mean it had a shallow end for the little kids like me and a deep end for the adults and big kids. It also had a diving board and lifeguards who wore uniforms. The most water I had ever jumped into, up to that point, was contained in the white ironclad claw-foot tub in our upstairs bathroom or the blow-up wading pool the neighbors had in their front yard each summer. So, as I stood on the edge of the Five Oaks Park swimming pool, it looked like an ocean of blue water. This moment became one of my most vivid flashes of memory from my early childhood.

I recall standing at the water's edge watching my neighbors and other children splashing about gleefully in the water. I just stood there apparently contemplating if I wanted to get in the water. It was at that point a big kid (maybe he was eight or ten years old) walked up to me and said, "Colored kids aren't allowed in the pool." I don't recall saying anything in response to the big kid. I just recall the mean look on his face and then looking back at the kids in the pool splashing about and laughing hysterically as they played in the water I was now forbidden to enter.

I began to cry. I cried so long and hard that when I looked down at my feet, I could not determine if the dampness on the pool's concrete edge was from the splashing of water from the pool or the tears I had produced from my eyes. It was at that moment I became aware of the fact that some people saw my uniqueness not as an asset, but as a liability. In one moment, this big kid who I did not know and who did not know anything about me other than my brown skin color had altered my trusted view of the world. That summer afternoon a river of tears obscured my trusted reality with doubt. The Lord intervened in the form of a pool lifeguard who came over to ask me why I was crying. I pointed to the big kid who was off laughing and talking with his friends. I told the lifeguard what the big kid had told me. He assured me that this was not true. I don't recall if I ever got into the pool that day. I think a part of me was wondering why the big kid felt the need to say what he had said if it were not true. Mommy had always told me that people are not supposed to lie. You don't get a cookie if you lie about stuff. I just recall the lifeguard making the big kid leave the park.

I would go on to have somewhat similar brushes with people or institutions who, despite obvious truths to the contrary, attempted to sow seeds of doubt about my life capabilities.

"You are not smart enough to go to college."

"You should just get a good factory job."

"You will never get into medical school."

What these distractors to the truth did not know was that hardwired within my DNA genetic blueprint was an incalculable belief in something greater than their inaccurate worldview of my capability.

Here is one final observation to ponder as I end this chapter. Have you ever noticed that no matter where you go on earth, or how primitive the culture you encounter, there is always a common belief in the existence of something greater than a mortal human entity or group of individuals? This essence subtly whispers to our spirit the answers of how we can make the impossible possible. It drives us to be curious about the unknown. It challenges us to seek the fullest capacity of our mortal existence. This essence is not bound by politics, finances, social status, cultural norms nor by the degree of pigmentation in our skin.

I have always been blessed with angels, like that lifeguard at the pool, who came to my rescue just in the nick of time with a message of encouragement. These earthly angels confirm that seeds of doubt can never grow if we do not give them the fertile soil of faithlessness to germinate.

—————

Don't stand on the edge watching others enjoy themselves, get into the pool of life and allow yourself to float in the direction you were intended.

Dream BIG and do not allow anyone on earth to extinguish your dream prematurely — not even you.

CHAPTER FOUR

"When we speak about how we feel about an event - this is gossip; when we report on what we think we observed - this is news; when society write about the residual evidence of the events - this is history. The truth is that only God will ever know the reality of what really happened."

"When I was God, I thought I knew everything." These nine words erupted from the edge of nowhere and collided with any conscious thought I was having at the time. I recall pausing to ponder the meaning of these words that were suddenly reverberating within my soul. Unlike the random arrival of quotes I had experienced in the past, these nine words did not reveal themselves to me as having a meaningful purpose. Despite this fact, those meaningless words continued to bang around the inner most crevices of my mind for the remainder of the day as if to dare me to acknowledge their need to be examined in greater detail. Weary of having my "inner voice" [Yes, I'm talking about that conscious little voice we have conversations with each day during our wakeful hours] dampened by the meaningless nine words, I paused at the end of my day to dissect the phrase.

"When I was God...." Well, this certainly seems like heresy. That was my first thought when this non-quote invaded my consciousness. I refused to acknowledge it and immediately attempted to dismiss its presence. There was nothing to see here, so I might as well move on to the next portion of the phrase.

But before I could move on, my thoughts challenged me to take a journey back to a point in time where few of us return. As I scribbled the first four words on the paper in front of me, I began to reflect on how I gained the **knowledge** to read and write these words. I thought to myself, "At what point in my life did I become **aware** of the purpose of a pencil?" This thought exercise took me back to some long-forgotten point in my childhood when I must have seen a pencil or a pen somewhere in our house and realized grown-ups used these objects to create less colorful images on paper than I could create with my giant size crayons. My thoughts pushed harder to try and recall my very first conscious thought as a human being. I recalled the first day we moved into my childhood home and seeing that apple-shaped cookie jar sitting on top of the tall white Frigidaire refrigerator.

The most distant memory I could retrieve from my conscious was of me sitting in my maternal grandmother's lap fascinated by a fat dark raised mole on the right side of her face. I could see myself as a child reaching up from her lap to touch the mole. As a teenager, I recall sharing this early recollection of my childhood with my mother. She questioned how I could have possibly remembered this event. Her mother had died unexpectedly of a stroke at the age of forty-nine shortly after my fourth birthday. However, when I told her about the mole on my grandmother's face, she confirmed my recall by fishing an old black and white Polaroid photograph of her mother from a box hidden beneath some old clothes in her dresser drawer. The fat black mole on the right side of my grand-mother's chin was not a figment of my imagination. Perhaps I did somehow salvage that morsel of toddler memory or per-haps as a curious child I had once found that same Polaroid photo while rambling through the dresser drawer, forgotten the event, and reimagined it as a discovered fragment of an actual interactive encounter I had with my grandmother.

Now it is your turn. Try as hard as you can to reacquaint yourself with that moment in your life when you first became **aware** of your own existence. As our genetically predeter-mined neuropsychological system matures into an adult con-sciousness it, much like a computer program, overwrites nonessential memories. It hardwires or imprints essential memories deemed necessary for the advancement of life and survival. So, even though I had no direct recall of when I first picked up a pencil, pen, or crayon to scribble on something there was a moment in time that I did so. In fact, there is still evidence of my early works of fine art on the unpainted walls at the bottom of the stairs of my childhood house.

I pushed further with my thought exercise to that point in my life where I imagined myself being born into a world as a genetically engineered and biologically viable human being with no retrievable memories available at birth to in-sure my survival. Without thought or demand, my every need was addressed. Everything external to me responded to my needs. When I felt the pain of hunger, I was fed. When I felt the discomfort of cold, I was comforted. When I needed love, it was provided unconditionally. I controlled the entire tiny world I knew. I existed in my world with no desires. My thought exercise pushed me back to this point in my life when I was closest to my creator. It was there where I had no peripheral desires or interferences to obstruct me from the **truth** of the world surrounding me. I was a blank canvas awaiting to be granted **wisdom** by a lifetime of human experiences. Suddenly, the nine words in my head clearly revealed a metamorphosis of meaning… "As God's creation, we desire to achieve wisdom."

"When we speak about how we feel about an event—this is gossip; when we report on what we think was observed—this is news; when society writes about the residual evidence of the event—this is history. The truth is that only God will ever know the reality of what really happened."

This quote no doubt arose after watching the news on television. I find it increasingly frustrating to consume modern era news without feeling violated or disenchanted about our prospect of survival as a human species. I know that is a boldly negative statement, but it is no longer the trusted news programming I grew up with. I could not put my finger on why I had become so angry and agitated by watching or listening to the news. Finally, I decided to do another thought exercise to analyze the source of my annoyance with the modern news media.

<hr />

We begin life as human creatures typically cared for by our biological mothers. Bonding to another human begins with our first oral meal from a mother's breast or a bottle. This

feeding routine evolves to the point the baby begins to imprint the image of the mother or trusted caregivers onto its
blank consciousness of understanding about the rapidly expanding world revealing itself to the infant. As we mature, we
are **educated** about our world by our caregivers and social environment. Within our first decade of life, this social imprinting becomes the cultural language we understand and the
genesis of that "little voice" speaking to us each day as we attempt to navigate society.

Early in our life journey most of us acquire a primitive
mode of transportation called crawling. This provides us the
opportunity to venture away from our primary caregivers and
acquire additional information regarding our surroundings.
With this ability to ambulate more freely in our environment,
the realization arises that the world is bigger than we had previously known. The crawler/toddler now discovers for the
first time that they do not know everything. Even worse, the
protective caregiver(s) restricts their access to obtaining new
information (i.e. preventing them from venturing down stairs,
climbing into cabinets, walking into traffic, playing with fire,
etc.). We hear the word "No" for the first time and repeatedly
thereafter. The toddler soon becomes aware of their restric-
tions in obtaining information about their expanding world.
This results in frustration, disappointment, tantrums, and
what we describe as the "terrible twos."

Eventually the harsh reality that we are not a god, whose
every wish and want will be fulfilled by others, is reconciled.
This usually happens by age four or five; but, unfortunately,
for some, this reality is not understood until much later in life

(i.e. adulthood). At this preschool stage of life, the child looks to those who provide them care as their authoritative source for the acquisition of knowledge. Instead of just physically touching, tasting, hearing, smelling, and seeing the world around them, children begin to ask the question, "Why?" Why is the sky blue? Why is snow cold? Why don't birds fall out of the air? Why do only mommies have babies? Why do people have to die?

When my youngest daughter, Ciara, was about five years old, she asked me, "Why do daddies know everything?" While I was both temporarily stunned and fascinated that she thought I knew everything, I resisted the urge to give her a humorous answer like, "Because daddy went to school, where he learned everything that there is to know." As I recall, I just looked at her and softly replied, "Only God knows everything, dear."

By age ten, most social character traits have been firmly imprinted on a child by the individual's family, geocentric culture, and social environment. Now, peers, friends, and mentors begin to supplant or supplement the parent(s) as a new resource for knowledge during the transition from adolescence to young adulthood. Despite the ever-present socially conscious "little voice" in our head telling us to do otherwise, a young person will sometimes do the opposite due to an overwhelming curiosity about the unknown or the pressure from peers to fit in or react to newly acquired hormonal instincts.

Until recently, this abbreviated description of early childhood development has been the usual course of human psychosocial evolution; but now a technological wild card has been thrown into this evolution of human psychosocial communication. It is called digital social media. Instead of knowledge transfer taking months, weeks, or hours to be transmitted, it happens instantly. Instead of waiting for the evening news or a morning newspaper, a summary of major news events appears in our life on our chosen social media device (cell phone, computer, digital pad, watch, or television) within seconds. We are bathed in the opportunity to consume new knowledge twenty-four hours a day. For some it has become a new form of addiction.

We no longer passively watch the news, we emotionally "feel" the news as it is visually presented to us. To increase viewer ratings, now the news is depicted more graphically. Commercials or political opinions come disguised as news. The desire to be the first to make a news story "go viral" often overrides the reporter's responsibility to verify all the knowable facts prior to distributing the information as legitimate news.

When we only speak about how we feel about an event— this is gossip:

"My cousin, Terry, got me addicted." He told me how much he enjoyed it, so I had to give it a try. It initially began with me going out to the car to turn on, but I found myself needing it every day. I began using it at home right there in front on my children. It was embarrassing, but I finally had to admit I had become addicted—to talk radio and television.

The appeal of this medium is how it resembles the familiar social chatter we hear at work, at the salon or barbershop, in the school lunchroom, or during dinner table conversations. Even if you don't have a water cooler at your place of employment most of us are familiar with the term "water cooler gossip." This is where we take a break from our daily work activities to hear detailed commentary about the latest office politics or scandals. During our adolescence, it was usually in the lunchroom or bathroom where our peers never even had to land a physical punch to invoke fear, anxiety, or major depression into some kid's life by spreading negative gossip about them. Now social media can be used as an instrument of mass character destruction by a new generation of cyberbullies who have the capability to spread fake gossip about our children within seconds.

When human feelings are used as the primary verifier of factual news, there is enormous latitude for erroneous observations to be made and transmitted to others in the disguise of factual news. Using traditional broadcast and digital social media offers what appears to be legitimate vehicles to share social gossip in the form of "opinion news." While it has its merits, it also provides a powerful tool to distort reality by injecting multiple layers of flawed observations, bias, prejudice, and unverified opinions. We exist in an era where we can find a media channel to validate or confirm any truth we elect to believe. [Author's note: This is not unique to the twenty-first century. Prior to this century we called them cults, sects, clads, exclusive social clubs, political parties, etc.].

Initially, I fell victim to talk media gossip. I found it was a great way to stay aware of what was happening in the world around me. Because it looked and sounded similar, I accepted it as being equivalent to the network produced news agencies I had traditionally consumed. I failed to realize that in our fast-paced news cycles there is limited time for trusted investigative journalism to occur. There is even less time for trained journalists to precisely filter legitimate news from social gossip. After noticing the many inaccuracies being delivered in the form of "Breaking News," I began the process of weaning myself from talk news media. It felt like a renewing breath of fresh air to not have my senses constantly bombarded by notifications from my phone, watch, radio, computer, newspaper, associates, television, and friends regarding what or who to be fearful of on any given day.

When we report on what we think was observed — this is news:

In ancient cultures, news spread by word of mouth. I'm certain gossip has been a mainstay of communication since humans have been able to use language to express their feelings about one another. However, before the printed word or books, most ancient cultures appointed a trusted elder to be the tribal storyteller. Notice how I used the word "trusted" to describe this individual who's in charge of providing the sacred history of their culture so it is accurately passed on to the next generation. Some of these individuals could recite centuries of historical information about their culture.

People transmitted history and news by way of parables, songs, religious hymns, stories, nursery rhymes, and various other means familiar to the culture. Most of us are familiar with the origin of the Olympic marathon distance of twenty-six miles and 385 yards. Dispatched from the battlefields at Marathon in 490 BC, the Greek messenger Philippides ran the entire distance of twenty-six miles and 385 yards to Athens, Greece to declare the Persians had been defeated. Legend also reports he spoke only three words, "We have won!" before collapsing on the floor of the assembly hall and dying. You could say this was the Golden Age of investigative journalism and reporting, when people were literally dying to spread the news. Philippides witnessed the Battle of Marathon and then reported the outcome without embellishment.

Hand printed logs of historical news events followed by the invention of the printing press in approximately 1450 largely supplanted the practice of exclusively using the art of storytelling. Those who had the ability to read and purchase books expanded their awareness about the world around them while the uneducated masses continued to rely on word of mouth or gossip as a means of spreading news.

Early after the turn of the twentieth century, radio became the new medium providing access to the news regardless of one's ability to read or write. All you needed to do was take the time to listen. It was not until the late 1940s that televisions became affordable enough to begin appearing in the average household. The National Broadcasting Company (NBC) briefly did a television simulcast of their radio network newscast in New York; but the Columbia Broadcasting System (CBS) was the first to pioneer a dedicated daily commercial news program to the nation. These technological advances brought the news from around the world directly into our homes at designated times. Everyone knew when legendary news anchor Walter Cronkite, aka "Uncle Walter," was on the television. Like most of his broadcast news colleagues, Cronkite was an investigative journalist who reported news facts and not his opinion. This earned him the honored title of "The most trusted man [person] on television." Thought exercise: What woman or man holds a similar title today?

As television matured, so did its ability to blunt our capacity to use our imagination. When there was only radio, listeners used their imagination to see the characters attached to the voices emitting from the "squawk box" sitting on the living room fireplace mantel or hidden in the dashboard of the family Chevy. As I listened to songs on the radio in my youth, I could only imagine what inspired the artist or songwriter to compose such beautiful music and lyrics. I used my own imagination to envision the characters and the scenery in the songs. Then came MTV (Music Television) with music videos. Seldom, if ever, did the videos match the scenery or the characters I imagined in my version of the song. Those videos were entertaining but not always lyrically accurate.

As the World Wide Web began to envelop our lives, social media began to supplant television and radio. Now the news could be in our home, in our pocket, and in our head (headphones) twenty-four hours a day. We can now post, Skype, Facebook, tweet, Snap Chat, email, and digitally gossip to the point of exhaustion. We literally have the means at our fingertips to spread our opinion, propaganda, virtual truth, unverified facts, or anything but the truth instantly. With great technology, that can become a weapon of massive societal destruction, comes great responsibility. Nothing but the verifiable truth is the threshold we should seek to achieve prior to hitting the Send button.

When society writes about the residual evidence of the event—this is history:

You may have noticed that in this chapter I injected a bit more researched history to demonstrate the value added in validating the truth provided by the storyteller.

A storyteller, whose purpose is to preserve an accurate history of their culture, takes pride in always choosing the righteous path toward preserving historical facts. The wise have no patience for idol gossip. Gossip can be corrupted by human emotion to alter the receiver's opinion of a person or group of people. Gossip is short-lived if not fed by public attention.

News is intended to accurately inform the masses of noteworthy, not trivial, events which someday may be worthy of historical memory. To become a good reporter of the news, an individual must demonstrate credibility. The individual does not have to hold the title the most trusted man or woman in broadcasting, but their professional work ethic and character should rise to a level that makes them worthy of the title. Let us define news as the raw evidence of human events happening in the present. Philippides was a warrior at the Battle of Marathon and thus had credibility when he reported the news, "We have won."

History is an amalgamation of social news events that have factually survived the scrutiny of time and social evaluations. History can be revised in the short-term, but the future will always reveal the truth. Gossip spread that the warrior Philippides ran into the Athens assembly building, then his lifeless body was brought out hours later. The news tells us the Greeks won the Battle of Marathon in 490 BC; but history confirms the Greco-Persian Wars persisted for another forty-one years (the war lasted fifty years from 499 BC until 449 BC).

Trusted storytellers or reporters of truth avoid participating in idol gossip or reporting unverified news. They seek to take what I call the "alphabetical path" toward wisdom.

This path begins with the desire to become **aware** of the truth. This is the reason children instinctively ask the question, "Why?" They desire to have an awareness of the truth. The wise know that all facts are not immediately known. To simply be aware that someone finds you attractive is not enough evidence to start making wedding plans. You must continue further down the "alphabetical path" toward wisdom before making the final decision to purchase wedding apparel.

Once the reporter is introduced to this void in their level of awareness, the pursuit of truth inspires them to seek trusted resources to **educate** themselves with factual evidence, not opinion, about the situation at hand.

With the appropriate amount of unbiased education, the learner will obtain true **knowledge** regarding how best to use this newly acquired asset to enhance their life or the lives of others.

Truth about the world around us becomes less complex when we have accurate knowledge. We become intellectually better equipped to anticipate how best to socially navigate our environment. The pursuit of truth becomes our guiding star to find a joyful serenity in life.

Wisdom comes when the reporter has gone through each of the above-mentioned steps. Then, they will have arrived at a well-researched, wise conclusion to integrate into their daily life.

When I was in medical school, I learned about the sympathetic nervous system. The fact that someone discovered this automatic physiological system in 1850 and named it after a basic human emotion—sympathy—was fascinating to me. This unseen autonomic nervous system works in concert with an opposing parasympathetic system to create a balanced neurohormonal environment that operates without our conscious knowledge. We do not have to think about breathing, making our food digest, or encouraging our heart to beat. When a fearful or confrontational situation is detected, the parasympathetic and sympathetic systems coordinate to activate the physiological mechanisms to facilitate either a "fight or flight response." Even love can be an activator (love sickness) or a stabilizer (to be in love) of this emotionally triggered system.

I began this chapter by expressing how I could not put my finger on why I had become so angry (fight) and agitated (flight) by watching or listening to the news. Through my thought exercises, I became aware of the subtle physiologic insult to my autonomic nervous system being activated repeatedly with unrelenting fear-invoking news. This constant neurohormonal overstimulation results in the breakdown of our primordial protective mechanisms and contributes to chronic disease (hypertension, diabetes, etc.), anxiety, depression, burnout, addictions, chronic fatigue, sleep disorders, and social dysfunctions. Try limiting the gossip, news, and non-work-related social media to less than one hour a day and replace it with an hour of silent contemplation. This daily dose of digital silence will literally allow your body to heal from the inside out.

We arrive on this earth with certain basic genetic, biological, and physiological assets that facilitate our survival. At some point, we become aware that we are unaware of absolute truth about the world around us. We are not a god who has all the answers. To experience truth, we must become as comfortable as the four-year-old who constantly asks the question, "Why?" Remember, our view of the world is filled with distorted perceptions we accept as fact because we have been imprinted with a lifetime of socially acquired beliefs — some being more accurate than others. Even in the presence of verifiable information, some of us will vehemently refuse to accept any facts contrary to their established belief. There are those who will decline any offer to journey down the laborious path from enlightened awareness to acquired wisdom. It takes time and the will to change the way we view the world around us.

I know I remember sitting in my grandmother's lap when I was three years old and touching that black mole on the right side of her face. The photo I may have seen in my mother's bedroom drawer had nothing to do with my recall of this event. The Polaroid picture just confirmed a fact I had not imagined — or did I? Only God knows....

━━━━

It is human nature to desire knowledge and truth about everything we encounter during our life journey. Some continue to pursue wisdom, while others stop the pursuit once they convince themselves that their version of the truth has been captured.

CHAPTER FIVE

"Destiny and fate will always offer us opportunities to change the status quo."

*W*hile sitting at my desk contemplating the origin of this quote, I suddenly felt a thirst for a bottle of cold sweet tea. Fortunately, I had purchased a bottle of tea earlier that same morning during a trip to the grocery store. There it was, just as I had left it, on the top shelf of my refrigerator nestled between the milk and orange juice. The only obvious difference from when I placed the tea in the refrigerator until now was the glistening hint of dew-like condensation covering the cool surface of the bottle.

Still distracted in thought, I removed the bottle of sweet tea from the refrigerator and attempted to set it on the kitchen counter. It was, at that moment, everything transformed instantly into one of those movie scenes where things move in slow motion. For several milliseconds my senses, memories, and unconscious thoughts unified in their focus on the following events…

As I pivoted from the refrigerator toward the kitchen counter, I could feel the dampness on the bottle's smooth dew-covered surface. That condensation caused my hand to slip just enough for the bottle to escape my tight grip. The bottle of sweet tea collided firmly enough with the counter's edge to jolt it out of my hand completely and allow gravity to take possession of the bottle's weight.

Immediately, I could sense my now empty hand communicating with my brain to stop daydreaming and begin evasive maneuvers. My gaze watched the bottle careening off the counter's edge toward the kitchen floor. Instantly a flash of probable outcomes erupted in my brain. In one scene, I saw the bottle crashing to the floor and the contents splashing from the shattered container. In another scene, I saw myself painfully injured by the heavy bottle that was accelerating toward my left shin and foot. It was far too late to realistically reach out and catch the falling object, so that scene never materialized in my consciousness.

Without any noticeable conscious thought, I extended my left leg into the path of the falling bottle. A falling glass bottle full of sweet tea would hit my tibia [shin bone] with such force as to certainly inflict a great degree of pain, but somehow my subconscious mind recalled the fact that when I purchased this particular bottle of sweet tea earlier in the day, I had noticed a subtle change in the product. Even though it looked like the other bottles of tea in my refrigerator, these new bottles of sweet tea were now made of plastic. Subconsciously, I had confirmed this fact from the weight of the container moments prior when I lifted it from the refrigerator shelf. My leg continued its extension into the path of the bottle creating a forty-five-degree angle, leg-to-foot incline for the plastic bottle to harmlessly bounce on and gently come to a spinning stop in the adjoining dining room. No broken glass. No injured leg. No river of sweet tea to clean up after the accidental drop.

This two-second event caused me to remember the genesis of the quote for this chapter. Years prior to this seemingly innocuous sweet tea encounter in my kitchen, I might have simply witnessed the status quo reaction to a bottle falling off the edge of a kitchen counter. If I could not catch the object in time, I would have simply moved out of the way, allowing the bottle to collide with the floor in order to prevent an undesired injury. However, on this occasion, a few deeply embedded experiential memories instantly offered me the opportunity to create an alternative outcome (fate) to an event by sequentially analyzing the many variables destiny had offered.

"Destiny and fate will always offer us opportunities to change the status quo."

As social beings, we invest a great deal of our lives into achieving a comfortable status quo. We often make compromising life adjustments to fit in with acceptable social norms. Achieving an acceptable social status or just classification as "normal" is the goal. Somewhere deep inside our labile consciousness there resides an intrinsic understanding of what it means to be normal. Perhaps some would define a "normal" human being as one who is in optimal physical, spiritual, and emotional health. This definition might also include a normal life as one where a sense of joy consistently resides within our spirit, and where we perceive no obstacles to achieving our imagined ambitions.

This may not be an appropriate definition of normality for all humans. However, it is reasonable to assume that most rational-thinking human beings have a desire to achieve some form of the socially accepted definition of "normal." To some degree, we can achieve this by making enough precise observations about the world where we exist to predict intuitively both immediate and remote life outcomes. If our acquired knowledge integrates correctly with our biological instincts and intuitive awareness, we can accurately predict life outcomes providing a sense of joyful tranquility. We feel normal when we can correctly predict outcomes.

Let's pause for a moment to do a thought exercise. Let's try to imagine a society where everything is predictable. No mysteries of life for solving. Nothing about which to be curious. No families wrestling with the terrible twos, adolescent unrest, or the stress of a mate struggling with midlife crises. No political disagreements or even the need for political parties because we are all on the same geopolitical page. No more desire for human warfare. Each of us would find our perfect "happily ever after" life partner on the first attempt. No longer would prejudice and envy cause emotional strife because our social resources would predictively provide for every member of society. The word "hope" would seldom be used in this imagined world where even the daily weather forecasts are accurate. Breaking news would be limited to those rare unpredicted events of fate occurring in society. In this world, a bottle of sweet tea falling off a counter and crashing onto a kitchen floor would be noteworthy as "breaking" news.

While to some this absurd imaginary world might seem desirable, this is not how we have evolved as a society. Because of the unpredictable nature of life, we, by necessity must learn new experiences and evolve in our knowledge of the unknown.

Because of our insatiable desire for knowledge, we have evolved in our ability to develop new communication technologies better equipped to predict the outcomes of socially disruptive situations. However, unpredictable natural disasters, political upheaval, acts of civil disobedience, and the presence of social discourse continue to be a modern-day Tower of Babel impeding our ability to create a precise, tranquil future where "normal" is the status quo.

A brief examination of history reveals a reoccurring theme of social chaos erupting as humankind made seismic psychosocial or major technological transitions to more advanced cultural norms. During these intervals of transition from the Bronze Age - through the Iron Age - the Middle Ages - the Renaissance - the Age of Enlightenment - the Agricultural Age - the Industrial Revolution - to the Modern Era, each was punctuated with major social discovery to enhance life, or military conflict where millions of human lives were lost. World War II was the deadliest military conflict in history. Over sixty million people (about 3 percent of the world's population at the time) died during this global military conflict. Despite having the benefit of objective history in our wake to assist us in forecasting these devastating outcomes, we continue to use primitive mental processes to repeat the same human error of social self-destruction; all because we desire others existing on our planet to fit into a model of what we perceive as the acceptable normal. "If only the rest of the world thought like me, it would be a better place to live." It would be very predictable. However, as we stumble through our current interval of cultural transformation, which some future historians may identify as the digital Information Age, we must use this information to avoid the same destructive tendencies of those who proceeded us.

Fate will always lead us to new destinies. It is our nature to be curious. Children are curious about their environment. This is how they learn and discover the world around them. As we age, however, some of us tend to lose our natural curiosity about life. Imagination wanes along with our desire to seek new possibilities. We get "stuck in our ways" of doing things. We become entrenched in our social bias based on personal or virtual (TV, radio, internet, social or print media) life experiences. Many of us allow opportunities and blessings to pass us by because we do not wish them to interrupt our routine rhythm of life.

Have you ever taken a different way home for some unknown reason and located a new restaurant that becomes a favorite? That restaurant would have remained undiscovered had you not listened to something in your spirit telling you to turn right at the next stop sign. Perhaps you were one of those individuals who was disappointed because you failed to get into your first choice for college and settled for your "backup." As fate would have it, you immensely enjoyed your college experience as it introduced you to a previously unimagined career opportunity, or better yet, your lifelong soul mate. Ask yourself, "Are the majority of your friends experiencing the life they expected to be living when they left high school or college?" On a more personal level, could you have imagined being where you are today twenty, ten, or even five years ago? If not, why not? Did fate reroute you to an unforeseen opportunity or a new destiny?

There are few coincidences in life. However, there are a sequence of fate-driven options offered to us during the course of our day. We select these options based on biological instinct, our experiential memories, inductive (intuition) or deductive reasoning, personal or virtual advice, a hunch, random chance, or by raw emotion. Fate can intervene at any ordinary moment to lead us to a devastating outcome or an extraordinary, life-altering blessing.

Why can't we turn away from a car wreck on the highway? Perhaps it is because the accident was an unexpected event intruding in our ordinary daily routine. It is astonishing that millions of us climb into our two-ton-plus vehicles and navigate them toward our respective destinations at speeds unimagined by previous generations of men or beast. We perform this feat using our stored memories and inductive reasoning to avoid colliding with other distracted motorists who are driving on emotional autopilot. In a rare instance, fate intervenes resulting in a misfortunate automobile accident. We come upon the accident and cannot resist the temptation to rubberneck. We witness a moment in the lives of the individual(s) involved. We feel for all the motorists subsequently impacted by the unexpected shared fate of the automobile accident. The little voice in our head asks us,

"Could the person in the mangled vehicle be someone I know?" You wonder how the accident happened. Perhaps there were fatalities. Some, just frustrated by the traffic delay, fear being late to their expected destination. Others in the resulting traffic jam are angry because fate placed them on this particular highway today. "I knew I should have taken that earlier exit," screams the little annoyed voice in your head. Nevertheless, we still slow down to look as we pass the scene of the accident.

Thus, here is the conundrum we struggle with each day. Our technologies have expanded exponentially since the dawn of the twentieth century, but the three-pound super computer each of us carries around in our skull has adapted at a much slower pace. No matter how amazing our brains are, our more primitive hormonal "fight or flight" protective mechanisms can override our brain's contemporary experiential logic capability rapidly.

These rudimentary neurophysiological functions transition us through various phases of stress alerts. Left unchecked, the constant presence of stress hormones circulating in our bloodstream damages our physical body. A medical doctor routinely cautions his/her patients to reduce the fat in their diet. However, I find myself advising my patients to take the FFATT out of their life as well. My meaning of the acronym FFATT is:

Frustration, Fear, Anger, Threat, Terror

The unpredictable nature of life results in reoccurring **Frustration**. Frustration is a common human attribute. I may become frustrated with my inability to solve a crossword puzzle. I am frustrated that my favorite sports team just lost a critical game. My car is making that strange sound again; that frustrates me.

At a grander level, I may also become frustrated because I have squandered an opportunity to achieve a lifelong dream because I made a poor decision. Frustration comes disguised in many forms. It can unexpectedly rob you of an otherwise perfect day. One moment you are living the dream; then in the next moment, you are on your knees mopping up your shattered [life] bottle of sweet tea.

The constant presence of challenging life circumstances heightens our curiosity to invent new and better methods to combat daily frustrations. A century ago, a person might have taken a day to ride a horse or the public stagecoach twenty miles to talk to a friend in the next county. Less than a half century later, that person could drive their car over to the friend's house in thirty minutes or less to have the same conversation. In today's world, losing even sixty minutes, to make that roundtrip to chat with a friend, can be too much time to spare. Now we have the capability to use cellular phone technologies from practically anywhere on earth to call and talk or video conference with friends and family within seconds. Certain social frustrations can assist us in our technological evolution.

Emotional frustrations left unchecked evolve into **fear**. "This final examination is far too difficult. I know I'm going to fail the test and flunk out of college." As fear creeps in from the darkest crevice of our conscience mind, logic begins its retreat. The increasing presence of the primitive neurohormones begins the process of corrupting the logic circuitry in the brain. As the stress neurohormones achieve a critical mass, our brain gives us the binary ultimatum of "fight or flight." Do I pause, take a deep breath and press on with the test [fight]; or do I tear the exam booklet in half, hurl its shredded remains to floor, and leave the room cursing [flight]?

In the example above, the presence of fear is the tipping point shoving us to the next phase of emotional deterioration. Was the examination too difficult or was I just not adequately prepared? The student felt trapped in a situation of her/his own creation. Given the absence of viable options, **anger** arrives to fill the void. Bathed by the increasing presence of stress hormones, anger can roam unleashed with no rational master of higher executive logic to tame it. Left unchecked, anger will reside in our spirit long after removal of the causative insult. Just think about this for a moment. Have you ever gotten so angry at a situation or at someone that hours, days, or even weeks later you "feel" as if something deep inside of you has been irreversibly damaged?

Unrelenting fear or anger pushes our capability to think logically over an emotional cliff into spiritual free fall. The anticipated crash introduces the presence of an overwhelming **threat** intruding into your life. At this point, your bloodstream is teaming with stress hormones. If this physiological situation persists over time, the individual begins to exhibit signs and symptoms of emotional overload, nervous breakdown, or physical burnout.

The last phase of this emotional train wreck is **terror**. At this point a virtual neuropsychological short-circuiting occurs. The fight or flight hormones are at a boiling point and the brain's logic functions are at their lowest point. The individual is "unconsciously" operating in an irrational fashion.

If an advanced society desires to avoid repeating the tragic errors of the planet's prior inhabitants, it must learn from their mistakes. Perhaps these earlier inhabitants lost their way by existing too long on the terrified axis of the FFATT equation. We may have more advanced technologies to relieve certain social frustrations but if we continue to live our lives in fear and anger, we will surely arrive in a state of threat and terror at an accelerated rate. Our social technologies can either result in an enhanced ability to strengthen our social relationships or hasten by proxy catastrophic and socially destructive outcomes.

Life events are not always a coincidence. The interweaving of our individual fates with the fates of others create a social fabric of opportunities. Social frustrations generate opportunities for the advancement of knowledge or emotional growth; however, a nation of people who have lapsed into angry debate have a limited capacity to extract themselves logically from a destiny of self-destructive behavior.

The winds of fate guide us to lands of uncertain opportunities. It is up to you to see past the accidental frustrations of daily life and allow faith to take you to a designated blessing. These blessings can appear as bottles of sweet tea landing unbroken on your kitchen floor, or as unplanned life-altering events that deliver you to unanticipated, joyful destinies beyond your status quo.

Blessings only become a reality if they are recognized and received.

CHAPTER SIX

"The ONLY genuine expert opinion of the future is one given by
someone who has been to the future and returned to the present to
reveal their personal experience of what tomorrow has in store."

$\mathcal{P}$repare, as the reader of this chapter, for a rather bizarre tale of a dream I experienced years ago. It is the genesis of this chapter's title...

As I recall, it was about three o'clock in the morning. Startled from my sleep, I struggled with my sheets as I sat straight up in bed. It was like a scene in a horror film. I had all the signs and symptoms of a panic attack. My pulse was racing at maybe 130 – 150 beats per minute. I could feel the sensation of my heart frantically pounding the inside of my chest cavity in an imagined effort to escape impending doom. I was breathing as if I were recovering from completing a competitive 100-meter sprint. I felt perspiration cooling on my damp forehead as my hands clutched my sweat-soaked bed linens. Through my dilated pupils, I looked out into the darkness engulfing my bedroom. The only interruption of the darkness was the dull ambience created by an alley's lamp about fifty yards behind my house. The streetlamp shined faintly through the curtained window directly behind my bed. As my vision adjusted, the silhouetted images of the larger objects in my bedroom came into view. Everything was as it had always been. Subconsciously, my biological defense protocols awakened, but I was safe from harm. Nothing had been disturbed in my room in that early morning hour — nothing except my thoughts.

I sat for a moment in the dark pondering what caused this unexpected emotional eruption. Suddenly, the vivid details of the dream I was having commenced to pour from my memory. The dream began with a vision of a young man, who was about my age, sleeping peacefully in his bed. His name was Malcolm. [**Author's note**: I have no recall of the character's name. I am fairly certain it was not Malcolm, but instead of just referring to him as "the man" I thought it would be better to provide him with a name.] Malcolm was abruptly startled from his sleep by a frightening dream or vision he experienced just prior to awakening. Panicked, he clumsily climbed out of bed and rushed to his bedroom window. There he stood in the dark looking into the distance at a little wooden cottage on a hill illuminated by the twilight's glow. Malcolm stared at the house as his mind took him back to the terrifying details of the dream that had shaken him from his sleep. In his dream, that same little wooden house on the hill was ablaze with fire that quickly reduced the structure and its lone occupant to ashes. His thoughts took him back to a time when, as a child, he wandered through the market in the town near the cottage.

Vaguely familiar with the spinster lady who lived in the hillside cottage, he knew she was kind to all those who knew her, but she was seldom seen participating in any social activities with other villagers. The elderly woman, who kept the little green and white cottage immaculate, was somewhat of a mystery. As far as everyone knew, she had always lived there alone. With no known living relatives, she had never married or been involved in any emotionally sustained relationships. Even the village elders could not recall an accurate history of how long the woman had occupied the cottage or from where she came. Her only known source of income seemed to be from selling the fruits and vegetables grown in her orchard and garden. She also sold beautifully crafted children's clothing at her stall in the town square market. This is how Malcolm knew the lady — as a child, she had made clothing for him. Even when he was a small child, the lady seemed old. He recalled having to stand for what in his child's mind imagined were hours while she took his measurements to create his school clothes for the season. As he forced himself to stand still to be measured, he would gaze into the lady's oddly youthful eyes. The iris color of her beautiful eyes reminded him of the light green limes she sold with the produce from her gardens.

Malcolm continued staring out his window up toward the lady's little wooden house. He recalled his dream of the house engulfed in flames. He had not really thought much about the lady — if at all — since he was well beyond the need of elementary school clothing. As an adult, he seldom accompanied his mother to market, so there was less opportunity to see the lady seated on her aged wooden stool in a market stall surrounded by fruits, vegetables, and the assortment of children's clothing she was selling. Before going back to bed, he wondered if he had this premonition because the old lady in the house was ill or dying. This thought continued to haunt him as he drifted back to sleep.

The next day Malcolm could not get the vivid dream to vanish from his mind. Toward the end of his workday, he decided to stop by the little cottage to check on the old lady. The sun was setting over the western horizon as he began his journey to the cottage. He had never before gone to the lady's house, but he was familiar enough with its location to find the path leading to her door. As a youth, he had walked near it on occasion. He and the other children even played hide-and-go seek near the orchards that lined the western edge of the hill where the cottage stood. However, he never had a reason until today to go to her home and knock on her door.

When he arrived, he took notice of the dilapidated wooden fence surrounding the cottage. The fence clearly hadn't been painted in years. The dirty white paint was peeling off in tiny sheets revealing the weathered gray wood beneath. Overgrown vegetable gardens surrounded the yard populated with an abundance of dandelions in various stages of maturity. Tall grass that chattered as it bowed in the evening breeze infiltrated the once well-groomed lawn. Malcolm walked guardedly up the brick walkway fearful of what he might discover in the house if he were to gain entry. As he approached the door, he mumbled to himself, "What if she is dead? What would I do then? Who would I tell?"

He stood at the doorway for a moment to compose his thoughts before firmly striking the green wooden door with his knuckles. Then he stood staring out into the distance patiently awaiting an answer. His ears heard the chilling whisper of approaching winds rushing across the old lady's yard. He looked back at the late day sun as it sculpted a beautiful cascade of light and color just above the orchard trees. The sound of the creaking green door opening interrupted Malcolm's random thoughts. The old lady stood staring at him with the same youthful lime-green eyes he remembered from long ago.

Silence lingered between them as the two once-familiar strangers examined one another by sight and thought alone. The silence ceased with the lady asking in a low sweet voice, "Can I help you, young man?" Malcolm seemed stunned to hear the familiar voice emerge from the individual standing inside the doorway. Yes, he recalled her sweet voice from a decade or so ago. Nothing about her had changed much other than a grayer head of shoulder length hair and a face with wrinkles that had deepened. She was the same sweet lady he remembered as a child.

Malcolm finally managed to ask, "Are you okay?" He saw the confused look on the lady's face as she pondered his question. Stammering, Malcolm added, "I mean, I know you probably don't remember me, but I just stopped by to see if you were okay… I mean, because no one has seen you at the market lately."

"I remember you, Malcolm," she replied. "I've been expecting you." Her words shot through Malcolm's brain for further processing. *It is amazing that she remembers me after all these years. Why on earth would she be expecting me to show up on her doorstep today?*

"Won't you come in?" the lady kindly asked Malcolm.

After a moment of hesitation, Malcolm stepped across the threshold of the cottage door. Mentally, he drank in the sight of the house's antiquities. Contained and stored within these walls were a lifetime of stories—hopes and dreams mixed with memories of tragedy and joy. All of this was palpably present as Malcolm surveyed the faded photographs and paintings on her walls. He noted the stacks of old books, papers and letters piled high on a walnut desk in the living room corner. In an opposite corner sat an ancient-looking black sewing machine with gold lettering written on its side. Surrounding the machine were piles of fabric and clothing. The air in the house had the musty odor of age. The odor was not overly offensive, but it smelled like a combination of old wood, stale urine, ancient papers, and decaying vegetation.

Malcolm continued to be preoccupied with examining the house as the lady asked if he wanted something to drink. "Oh sure," he responded. The lady disappeared from Malcolm's view, into the adjacent kitchen, to apparently get him the drink. They each raised their respective voices to continue their conversation.

From the kitchen, Malcolm heard the lady's voice over what sounded like cans or pans banging beneath a cabinet. "You said that you wanted to know if I was okay. What made you stop by after all of these years to check on me, Malcolm?"

He was uncertain as to whether he should be evasive or truthful about the reason for his visit. He thought to himself, *She will think I'm crazy. The truth might even frighten her to death.*

After some thought, Malcolm finally summoned the courage to tell her about his dream. He shared with her the graphic details of the tragedy he witnessed in his nightmare. "I just could not get the thought of that dream out of my head all day. So, I just had to stop by to check on you."

As Malcolm listened for her reply, something outside the living room window caught his attention. Through the thin linen drapers, he could see down the hill into the town. There, at the outskirts of town, Malcolm could see the bedroom window of his house where earlier that morning he had been looking up at the little house in which he now stood. He recalled the nightmarish horror of seeing the cottage engulfed in flames.

Malcolm no longer heard noises emitting from the kitchen. Still staring out the cottage window, he heard the lady reply in a raised voice. "That was very kind of you, Malcolm, to stop by and check on the old lady today." The slight giggle that followed her comment brought a smile to Malcolm's concerned face.

As Malcolm continued to reflect upon his twilight dream, he recalled the sadness he felt knowing the old lady had perished in the flames alone. As he continued to look into the distance at his bedroom window. Malcolm cleared his throat and spoke loudly, "Why were you expecting me today?"

Suddenly, a new aroma permeated the musty odor of the cottage. Malcolm felt the moisture of liquid seeping through the clothes on his back. It was as if time stood still. All his senses became intense and focused. He recognized that smell, it was kerosene. Had the lady spilled some kerosene in the kitchen? As he turned away from the window to look toward the kitchen, the lady, standing about three feet away from him. blocked his view. Just as she splashed fluid onto his chest, he saw the metal container in her left hand—the container holding the kerosene. Stunned, Malcolm recoiled backward toward the window. With the palm of his right hand, he felt the coolness of the glass in the window pressing against him.

Unable to step back any further Malcolm was now about four feet away when he saw the lady strike a wooden stemmed match and hold it in front of her. It illuminated the dim room. Her lime-colored eyes reflected the flickering yellow, orange, red match light. Just as she dropped her flaming match on the kerosene-covered floor, she spoke one last time. "I didn't die alone in the house fire, Malcolm. I don't know how you saw into my future, but now my past and your future are here in the present."

"The ONLY genuine expert opinion of the future is one given by someone who has been to the future and returned to the present to reveal their personal experience of what tomorrow has in store."

If a prophet foretelling your future knocked on your door, would you let them in? Most of us would think they were crazy and demand they go away. However, we consistently seek knowledge about the future everyday through statistical analysis, scientific forecasts, advice columns, social media, gossip, horoscope predictions, expert opinion givers, and self-proclaimed modern-day prophets who have never been to the future. Our biblical, historical, and fictional literature offers us numerous stories of people who somehow have defied the linear march of time by accurately glimpsing into the future. For some, their heralded ability to see beyond the present ultimately resulted in significant societal changes. Most view these future tellers as flawed eccentric misfits during their season of life on this earth.

So how is it that throughout the ages these social misfits somehow see through the conventional wisdom of their era to dream about the future in unconventional ways? In 1510, Leonardo Da Vinci, a self-educated artist and sculptor, correctly described the physiology of how blood flows through the human aortic heart valve — 450 years before it was scientifically confirmed in the 1960s. How did Isaac Newton, a seventeenth-century farmer's son, watch apples fall from trees to the ground (there is no evidence that any of the apples hit him in the head) and subsequently dream up the laws of motion and universal gravity? How did a couple of high school-educated brothers (Orville and Wilbur Wright) from my hometown of Dayton, Ohio, without benefit of any formal aeronautical training, design and successfully fly the first heavier-than-air plane in 1903? They did so without the financial support of private investment firms, the encouragement of the US government, or the direct input of visionaries who tried before them. How could a young unknown patent office worker, Albert Einstein, come up with "the world's most famous equation" $E=mc^2$ without divine intervention? In the 1960s, visionary Rachel Carson, authored the landmark book, *Silent Spring*, igniting a world environmental movement. While in the same timeframe, a Baptist minister from Atlanta, Georgia dreamed of creating a civil rights movement fueled by a commitment to peace and unity.

I was a teenager when I experienced the actual dream depicted in the introductory paragraphs of this chapter. It haunted me for weeks. Even as I wrote the details of my dream for this chapter, I could still feel a residual element of uneasiness lingering in my soul. **Reality check:** I never knew an old lady with eyes of lime green, and I never lived in a village below a green and white cottage on a hill. I certainly never went up in flames in a house fire. The closest I ever came to a house fire was my mother telling me about how the family rooming house (where we lived prior to moving to my childhood home on Williams Street) caught fire when I was a toddler. She shared her story of how, while escaping the fire, she fell in the snow with me in her arms. My mother saved both of our lives, in a literal sense, that night. Had it not been for her actions on that fateful night, I might have perished alone in that huge green and white rooming house.

The quote for this chapter appeared from out of nowhere many years after my twilight dream. I suspect a lifetime of well-meaning individuals attempting to provide me with sage advice about what my future had in store may have prompted it. Granted, much advice handed down from generation to generation is to provide the younger generation with objective guidance regarding what life obstacles to avoid. This practice of using known social history to forecast probable future outcomes provides our youth with an opportunity to avoid making the same mistakes of earlier societies or their parental guardians. Even in the most primitive societies there is always an elder charged with recording the history of their community. In other words, people within a community perpetuate a "common unity" of thoughts, experiences, ideas, dreams, or ambitions as a method of preserving the collective memories of their existence on Earth. We pass on common unifying principles to offspring in hopes of insuring the survival of their culture.

We typically rely on these preserved historical chronologies to predict future outcomes. These past and recent experiential events provide society with credible predictive evidence on how the future is likely to evolve. This pattern of using the past to predict the future is sufficient except in the rare instance when, through an apparent gift of divine providence, bestowed visionary knowledge gives a member of the community the ability to warn us of a need to depart from conventional wisdom. These geniuses or prophets of events to come provide us with a glimpse into a yet-to-be confirmed future.

In its most basic form, proven information gleaned from past or recent events is the basis for "good advice." Experiences, not yet experienced, can't be used to predict how to conduct our life in the present. This would seem to be common sense, but how often do we find ourselves making critical life decisions in the present based on what we plan will occur in the future? When X happens, I will do Y and that will equal my desired outcome (XY). In this **life algebra,** the unknown variable X is the future. How many times have you heard someone state, "When I meet the right man/woman, things will be better, but until then I don't need to worry about saving money." You could replace "meet the right man/woman" or "saving money" with thousands of other inserted phrases. We don't know what we don't know about the future, but many of us act as if we have full knowledge of expected events of tomorrows yet to come.

In our modern age, we no longer rely exclusively on a closed, unified community of people to guide our future life experiences. We can obtain random advice from multiple external sources. Why, in fact, with the flip of a remote control, we can select the source of the advice we want to saturate our consciousness. With a universe of choices, it becomes increasingly difficult to know what advice to use confidently to navigate life's anticipated obstacles.

One rule of thumb I have provided to my children — always hit the mental Pause button when someone attempts to provide you with sage advice. While on pause ask yourself three questions: 1.) Why does this person want you to believe their advice? 2.) Is this advice based on verifiable past or present experiences? 3.) Will the individual giving the advice receive any personal gain by you acting upon their advice? If the advice is based on the possibility of future events (e.g., if horse #7 wins the race you will become rich), be suspect. Like supplying nutritious food, only dispense advice if it improves the overall vitality of the consumer.

Homework Assignment: So much of our 24/7 news cycle consists of predictions of future outcomes provided by "expert commentators." Let's verify how precise our experts are at glimpsing into the future. Go to your local library or the archived internet files of your favorite newspaper, radio/television station, or the social media site. Find a few expert opinion feeds from one year ago. Verify the precision of the media site in predicting the future we now live in. If your homework identifies a media site that accurately scores greater than 70 percent in their predictions, this is a reliable source of factual news.

Could you imagine a news channel with the tag line: "We don't let facts get in the way of the reality we want you to believe"? Now that would be truth in advertising. Intentionally disguised as a legitimate source for information, entertainment news programming is contaminated with subliminal unproven opinions, hearsay, political spin, embellishments for ratings and is frequently produced by persons with clandestine personal agendas.

On the other end of the information spectrum are those who some would classify as eccentric reporters of future events. Unlike their media counterparts, these individuals are difficult to identify because they seldom reveal themselves to their respective societies. These divine prophets of the future humbly reside in ordinary social situations. Because of their unrelenting curiosity about the world surrounding them, they retrieve brief glimpses of how the future is likely to unfold. Where others only see ordinary daily occurrences, these social outliers simply make extraordinary observations of existing social systems. These glimpses into the future can be sparked in the spirits of individuals who, because of personal or social challenges, lead society to a better future out of the necessity to change the status quo because we can no longer do the same old thing. A sudden, vivid dream of how life can improve ignites prophetic insights that become an awakened reality.

There are no mortal experts on what precisely will occur in the near or distant future. Life is certainly uncertain. Therefore, we each should dare to be more like those unconventional historical figures who provided humanity with a glimpse of things to come through the trifocal lens of their past-, present-, and future-focused observations. What these contemporary prophets of change and pioneers of hope had in common was their ability to see an incomprehensible future just beyond the horizon of their era's conventional wisdom. No visionary who has seen the future could comfortably return to the present with a desire to rely only on the once unquestioned knowledge of the past. This discomfort is precisely what makes them appear to be misfits among their contemporaries.

Unlike Malcolm, not everyone who glimpses into the future falls victim to tragedy. He knocked on the old lady's green wooden door expecting to intervene changing her future by sharing the details of his dream. Instead, he became an unsuspecting participant in her present-day activity of destroying herself and all her memories. The future he had foreseen remained unchanged. Malcolm had faith in his ability to change someone else's future using unverified future facts presented to him in a vivid dream. If he had only also taken the time to focus his present observations on the weeds in the garden, the odor of rotten food in the house, the piles of unfinished clothing, her absence from the market place. These observations would have provided him with additional important intuitive glimpses into the future regarding the desperate state of the lady who had occupied the once immaculate little cottage. Had he been less preoccupied, recalling the past events of his twilight dream, while looking out the window at his own house back down the hill, he might have remained present in the moment. Being present in the moment could have created a different future for both he and the old lady with the lime-green eyes.

Dreams are a byproduct of our brain's neurotransmitter regulation process. These functions collide with random collections of subconscious experiences activating and deactivating synaptic receptors within our cognitive command center during the rapid-eye movement portion of our sleep cycles. In a rare instance, something erupts from this neurological chaos when a new idea for a grander future invades our conscious mind. It can make you sit straight up in bed with your biological "fight or flight" protocols subconsciously awakened, only to discover you are safe from harm. During that early morning hour, nothing has been disturbed in the room except possibly your future.

-◦▬◦▬◦-

The future is not promised, nor is it something to be feared. Do not be disturbed from your slumber by the arrival of the future. Be joyful for yet another day of life. Be grateful for the opportunity to increase your experiential knowledge. Do not fear the future. Have faith in the many blessings waiting there for you.

CHAPTER SEVEN

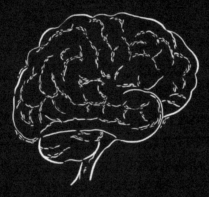

"You have to go past knowledge and truth in the dictionary before you arrive at WISDOM."

$\mathcal{B}$efore you begin this chapter, pause for a moment to turn off all of the external visual and auditory distractions that might interfere with your reading of this introductory story. Good. Let's get started.

Now try and recall how vibrant your imagination was when you were a child. Left in an empty room with no television, phone, computer, or interactive toys, a child can use their imagination to create a spontaneous world filled with fantasies and wonderment.

Engage your vehicle of imagination to begin a journey to a time when the earth was much younger. You arrive in a land far away from your present existence. There you see two young siblings running in the green meadowlands of their family farm. This is the scene where our story begins…

These happy children are almost inseparable because, as fate would have it, the younger sister, at an early age, had become blind. She depended on her older brother to be her eyes in a world she could no longer visually perceive. The older brother took great pride in caring for his little sister. Together they roamed the meadows surrounding their farmhouse. They spent hours exploring the mysterious caves that laced the mountain range bordering their land.

Unfortunately, for the family, the wealthy property owner who owned all the land adjacent to their farm had forbidden anyone to trespass on his acreage. As a result, to avoid crossing the neighbor's land, the family had to spend an extra day of travel when journeying to the closest village to sell the family's harvest. In their youth, the brother and sister chose to ignore the demands of the wealthy neighbor. For years, they fished in his lakes, climbed his hills, and, using homemade torchlights, they explored the mountain's eminent caves. This angered the landlord because, although his servants informed him of these intrusions on his property, they could never capture the youngsters.

As the brother and sister matured, they realized their parents were growing too old to travel the long distance to the village to sell crops. They knew it was time for them to assume the responsibility for delivering the harvest to the town market. The parents reluctantly agreed. As they loaded up their wagon and set out on their journey, the siblings secretly agreed to take the forbidden, shorter route through a portion of their neighbor's property. They knew the landlord was far too old and feeble to capture them.

The siblings arrived in the village and conducted the family's annual business of selling the crops for a handsome sum of money. Anxious to get home to inform their parents of what they had accomplished, they decided to take the same forbidden route home not realizing that the landlord's relatives were lying in wait.

On their return trip home, the two were robbed, beaten and taken to the landlord who would decide their ultimate fate. Pleased with the capture, the landlord sternly gave them a choice.

Beating his chest with a closed fist, he growled, "You have taunted me for years, but now your lives are in my hands. The choice is yours. My men can take you to the high cliffs overlooking the valley where they will cast you off the edge, causing a quick and painless death; or I can have them take you into the depths of the caverns that lie within the mountains. There you will slowly die of thirst and starvation or be devoured by the beasts that roam in the darkness of the caves."

Without awaiting the counsel of his sister, the brother announced his decision of banishment to the caves. He thought to himself, "This is our best chance for survival because we explored those caves many times as children." Surely, they could eventually escape from the darkness of the caves. He also knew the existence of beasts roaming in the caves was unproven folklore.

Prior to their exile to the caves, the brother cunningly asked the landlord if he would grant them one request. He asked if they could somehow manage to escape the dangers of the cave, would the landlord promise to give his family title to all of the land laying between their farm and the village? In the presence of all his relatives, the landlord laughed and agreed to the terms, confident he would never need to fulfill this promise. He knew this was the last he would ever see of these two pesky siblings.

The servants of the captors did not know the extent of the sister's blindness so they blindfolded both young captives and led them deep into the caves. They warned the children that they were not to take their blindfolds off and attempt to follow the light of their captor's torchlights to escape. If they removed their blindfolds, the servants had orders from the landlord to immediately slay them with the well sharpened daggers they had each been provided for the task.

When they no longer heard the footsteps of their retreating captors, the brother instructed his sister to stay put while he set out to find safe passage to the exit. Although blindfolded, he sensed having previously traveled on the trail his captors followed when depositing them in the cave. Just as he suspected, the armed servants had unwittingly taken the siblings down one of the many trails he and his sister had explored as children.

At this point, he removed his blindfold to verify that the servant's torchlights were gone and it was safe for him to begin his trek. He looked around and all he could see was darkness. He had never witnessed such darkness. He lifted both hands from the cold stone floor of the cave and placed them in front of his face. He knew the position of his hands, but his brain perceived only an impenetrable curtain of darkness. Fear became the formidable beast in the cave. The brother groped to his feet again instructing his sister to wait at her current location as he looked for the exit. He heard his voice echo off the invisible walls of the cave as he said to his sister, "Don't be afraid. I will be back for you."

After going only a few yards, he stepped into a rut in the cave's floor and fell. His next few steps forward caused him to slam into a solid object protruding from the ceiling of the cave. In his youth, he recalled seeing many of these obstacles that were easily avoided when illuminated by a torchlight's flame. They resembled the winter ice sculptures hanging from the edge of the home he was hoping someday to see again. The beast of fear continued to pursue him through the deep darkness.

He thought to himself, Is this what my sister has lived with every day since she became blind? After several attempts to move in the darkness, he repeatedly met with unseen obstructions that blocked his advance forward. Tears began to fall from his face as he realized they would never escape their dark prison. He cried out for his sister saying, "I have failed you and our parents. Surely we will now die in this darkness."

As the now physically and emotionally injured brother lay weeping on the cold dark floor of the cave, he felt something touch him on his shoulder. Startled, he looked about in the dark thinking it was one of the mythical beasts seeking to devour him. He lay facedown on the cold stone of the cavern floor expecting the beast's teeth to penetrate his flesh and seal his fate. Instead, he heard his sister's sweet assuring voice saying, "Don't be afraid, dear brother, I know the way home. Together we can find our way back to your light." You see, unlike her older brother, she was not fearful of the darkness nor was she crippled by it. She could use all of her other human senses to their full capacity to find the way to freedom. It was the sister, not exclusively dependent on **the torchlight**, who actually had the greater vision.

Together, they eventually emerged from the cave. Their parents, who had been informed of their banishment by the landlord, greeted them with cheers and celebration. As promised, the family took ownership of the land providing thoroughfare to the village. As the landlord signed over the deed to the land, he paused to ask them, "Without the torch's light, how did you find your way through the darkness of the cave? What or who led the way to your freedom?"

"You have to go past knowledge and truth in the diction- ary before you arrive at WISDOM."

Both the short story about the two lost siblings and the quote for this chapter came to me from the edge of nowhere. For no particular reason my imagination began to produce brief scenes of two young farm boys. (**Author's note:** In the original version of the story, there were two brothers riding with their parents to market on an antiquated wooden wagon filled with baskets of produce). Over the next several days, my daydreams of the tale expanded to two brothers, who after playing in the sundrenched meadows of their farm, paused for rest atop the soft, freshly harvested wheat. There they both shared their respective hopes and dreams for the future. Their fate and the choice of the cliff or the cave was an unsettling twist to an otherwise joyful tale.

As I recall, the quote for this chapter arrived many years after my daydreams of the two children lost in the cave. One day I was looking up a few definitions in my tattered paper- back dictionary. While rummaging through the dictionary pages, the quote just dropped into my consciousness. It later reminded me of the story involving the farmer's children. It took me back to the final questions of the angry landlord. "Without the torch's light, how did you find your way through the darkness of the cave? What or who led the way to your freedom?"

Back in an earlier chapter (Chapter 4), I provided the reader with an advanced glimpse of things to come by introducing the path our thoughts must follow to arrive at conscious wisdom. Let's expand on what was written earlier using the tale of our two siblings lost in the cave's darkness as our guide.

Those seeking wisdom are best served by taking a proverbial route I will refer to as the **"alphabetical path toward wisdom."** This path begins with the letter **"A" Awareness:** It is wise to always have a genuine desire to become **aware** of the truth. The two children in our story had a natural desire to expand their awareness of a world existing beyond the borders of their little farm. This youthful curiosity led them to explore their farm and its neighboring properties.

Driven by an unconditional love for his younger sister, the elder sibling accepted the responsibility of being her caretaker. He viewed tending to his visually impaired sibling as a privileged commitment to his family. Through this bond as children, they together discovered the caverns beneath the mountains on the neighboring landlord's property. This same curiosity sparked the ingenuity necessary to create the homemade torches. These torchlights lit their way as they explored the cavern's depths in search for hidden treasures.

Together they enjoyed adventures sneaking onto their neighbor's land and disappearing into the bowels of the dark caverns. The children could not have imagined their fate of someday being left in the caves to die. With each journey through the caves, the siblings became keenly **aware** of each unique path coursing through the darkness. By the light from their torches, the older brother safely guided himself and his sister along the sloping paths leading into the mysterious depths of the mountain's underbelly. He became adept at using his eyes to identify landmarks and obstacles to avoid on each path.

As he led the way, he was unaware his unsighted sister perceived a different journey than his own. Using her enhanced ability to listen as they traversed the various paths, she heard the cave speak to her through sound variations caused by the terrain beneath their feet. Differences in the types of echoes reverberating from the massive stone walls announced their arrival in yet another hollow chamber of the mountain. Her sense of smell alerted her to the presence of spring water seeping from unseen crevices in the stone. She could detect the scent of vegetation growing as they neared the opening of the caverns. Unlike her sighted brother, she became accustomed to feeling subtle transitions in temperature at various depths of the cave. As she trailed along the paths, she felt a conscious enjoyment when gentle currents of wind coursed through the darkness breezing by her face. Faith in her brother's vision caused her to allow him always to take the lead as she **educated** herself about what she could not see.

The capacity to be more observant, and thus more aware of information, does not immediately deliver the observer to the altar of wisdom. We cannot linger at awareness alone; we must continue further along the "alphabetical path" toward wisdom before making final decisions on how best to proceed in life.

Once introduced to previously unknown information, our newly found awareness should inspire us to seek the next landmark on our journey toward wisdom. **"E" Education:** Use personal experiences or trusted resources to **educate** ourselves further about what we think we now know. By using factual evidence — not speculative opinions — we can integrate new information into our past and current life experiences to create a more precise view of anticipated future events.

How many of us have read the entire sacred book (i.e. Holy Bible, Koran, Torah, Upanishads, etc.) of our chosen religious belief? Some of us act as if we have. Without fully educating ourselves, we may unintentionally quote scripture out of context, speak with authority without true knowledge, teach others unsubstantiated information, or follow religious doctrine as if we were wholly educated about every word printed within the sacred document's bound covers.

As the brother and sister in our story grew into young adults, they educated themselves about how to run their parents' farming operations. By giving them "chores" to do, their parents taught them the ethics of work. The children observed how their father tilled the fresh soil each spring. While kneeling in the fields, their mother instructed them how to properly plant seeds in the earth. She taught them to distinguish weeds from young emerging crops. Through the repetition of experience, the children educated themselves on how to tend flocks and prepare crops for harvest. As young adults, they sought to validate their education by volunteering to take the harvest to market. However, in their youthful exuberance, they unwisely decided to take an illegal shortcut to and from the village. This ultimately resulted in their capture and imprisonment in the darkness of the cave.

With an appropriate investment in applied educational theories, the learner soon arrives at the next important landmark on the route toward wisdom. **"K" Knowledge:** Obtain a critical mass of comprehensive education about a topic before achieving verifiable **knowledge** regarding the subject under study. Newly acquired knowledge is an invaluable asset. It can be stored away for anticipated or unanticipated future use. This new knowledge can be an invaluable asset in enhancing one's personal life and/or the lives of others seeking similar knowledge.

Although the older sibling understood the cave's darkness and educated himself on how safely to navigate the cave's perilous architecture, he had insufficient knowledge in total darkness. With the constant aid of their torchlights, he had no need to educate his human senses how to adjust for the total absence of light in the deepest depths of the cave. Without the presence of light, he had no remaining sensory resources capable of freeing himself and his sister from the bondage of the darkness. This unanticipated event forced him, for the first time in his life, to share the bondage of blindness his sister had known for most of her life.

The **"T" Truth:** The quintessential milestone on our path toward wisdom, the truth about what we perceive in the world around us is less complex when we have accurate information to make informed decisions. In the presence of truth, we are better equipped to navigate our social environment. The pursuit of truth should always be the guiding star by which we search for serene joy in life.

In our story, it was the younger sister who had acquired a subtle, but more comprehensive, form of knowledge during the siblings' many journeys down the cave's darkened paths. She knew the concealed **truth** regarding the nature of the caverns. Fear of the unknown can poison our ability to use our acquired knowledge to think logically. Because the younger sister carried a concealed truth within her, she was not fearful, angered, or terrified by the grip of darkness surrounding them.

Only at the finish line do we feel the embrace of **"W" Wisdom:** There are no easy detours to this destination. In our daily lives, people often expend a great deal of energy in an attempt to convince us that achievement of wisdom requires minimal personal effort. Others will attempt to convince the masses how they alone have found a viable shortcut to the secrets of life. Do not be fooled by such pronouncements.

At the end of our story, it wasn't the older brother who led the sibling pair to safety. It was the younger sister who, over the years, acquired a special **wisdom** as she passively followed her brother's lead. Without the aid of the torchlight, it was the sibling, without benefit of vision, who led her injured brother back through the darkness into the outstretched arms of two grateful parents waiting at the cave's opening.

How can anyone find wisdom without first achieving an awareness about the deficit of knowledge? How can anyone acquire knowledge without a willingness to educate themselves with facts? How can anyone achieve an education of enduring value without verifiable truth as its foundation? Only after we have gone through the progressive steps on the "alphabetical path" can we arrive at the final destination where wisdom awaits. Dare to take the unconventional path through life. Misfits among us who walk on a path toward wisdom clearly see a future shrouded from the eyes of those trapped in the darkness of a social status quo.

Sometimes life's circumstances lead us down paths we dare not go voluntarily, only to deposit us into seemingly inescapable situations. We can choose to sit in the darkness seeking salvation by screaming out that we have lost our way; or we can call upon our higher inner vision of faith. With hope, faith, and knowledge, we can stand up to the unseen obstacles of our existence to emerge victorious at a bright, unimagined destination.

***

Just because something can't be seen is not verification of its absence. Notice the wind. It is invisible; however, we see the presence of its might and power.

Some of life's most precious gifts are within our midst but remain unnoticed if we do not have the wisdom to see them.

CHAPTER EIGHT

"Promise nothing but act as if you have."

ot all artistic epiphanies arrive from the edge of no-where. Sometimes bouts of creativity interrupt our conscious thoughts, like an unavoidable yawn; a pleasant rhythm; lyrics to a song never sung; a clever plot for an unwritten novel; an idea for an unimaginable work of art; or the simple animation of a poet's pen.

I enjoy reading biographies about ordinary people who gain notoriety by creating extraordinary works of art, literature, scientific discovery, or social activism. A common theme in the majority of these historical life stories is that the most noteworthy accomplishments seem to emerge from out of no-where. While sitting in solitude beneath an apple tree near his mother's home, Sir Isaac Newton's consciousness gave birth to the revolutionary theory of gravitational acceleration. The simple act of passively watching apples fall to the ground — and not on his head, as legend has it — was his inspiration. Songwriters often tell stories of how the melody for a musical standard suddenly came to mind while taking a quiet walk or relaxing in some hole-in-the-wall hotel room between gigs.

Hastily written by hand on scraps of paper, many iconic works of music and literature originated when an inspirational thought arrived unexpectedly. President Lincoln scribbled 272 words on a piece of paper while in route to Gettysburg, Pennsylvania the outcome of which resulted in delivery of one of the most memorable speeches in American history.

Often a mixture of **solitude, silence, and simplicity** serves as essential elements to hearing divine voices of creativity whispering from the distant edges of nowhere.

Instead of beginning this chapter with a story, I am sharing a short poem I received spontaneously and wrote within minutes without even knowing its meaning or purpose. It was unbelievable…

Read it to see how you interpret the words. Then read it a second time to see if it conveys the exact same meaning. At the conclusion of the chapter, I will deconstruct the poem to share my thoughts on its meaning.

Unbelievable

Here I am,
    I'm unbelievable;
Invisible,
    I'm inconceivable.
Truth be told,
    No one here will care or ever notice;
Just stick to the plan,
using the status, they all are required to quote us.

Yeah, look at me,
    I'm so unbelievable;
When I speak, I try to raise my voice,
    To drown out deceptions and give the believers an actual choice.

I speak few words hoping that someone will hear a thing or two,
    Wasting time creating broken rhymes about real times as if I have a clue;
These spoke words are seldom heard,
    Because no bodies on earth are really listening to you.

I want you to love my good, flaws, and ugly,
    Because that's all a part of me;
Yeah, I'm so unbelievable
    But that's what I strive to be.

I tell them facts to see how they will react,
    I've been told that facts don't ever lie;
We've all been told truth is good for something,
    But there are those out there who ask me why.

I'm right here for you,
    I'm unbelievable;
      My presence here is not so unconceivable.
My momma told me, "boy you should never lie."
But when I speak the truth, you never cease to ask me why.

The truth is not always recognized by the eyes of those who blindly receive it,

Is it so overwhelming we can never comprehend, check it out, or dare to believe it Here I am I'm not so invisible;

Here I am — I promise — I'm not unbelievable.

"Promise nothing; but act as if you have."

How many times have you listened to a conversation, and the person prefaces their comments by saying, "To tell the truth... " or "To be perfectly honest with you..."? Every time I hear either of these phrases, I subconsciously ask myself, *What? Have they been lying to me up until this point?* This is especially distressing if the person talking is attempting to convince me to alter my way of thinking about an important topic or is trying to sell me something of reported value.

I suspect it is the intent of the speaker to use these phrases to place the listener on alert that the statements soon to follow are undeniably valid. It is their way of "promising" that the truth being shared is accurate.

As social creatures, we value truth telling. Elders and parents teach their children to tell the truth at all times. We learn very early in life the consequences for distorting facts, intentionally attempting to deceive others, or telling a big fat lie for personal gain. Parents physically and/or emotionally punish children when they lie. This punishment can come in many forms: a verbal tongue-lashing by your adult guardian; a spanking; a slap upside the head; being grounded or placed in timeout; being denied use of a favorite toy or television privileges; or being sent to bed without dinner. These punishments, some socially accepted and others inappropriate, sequentially imprinted the value attached to truth telling.

Educating all members of society to tell the truth consistently and to value following agreed upon directives creates a sense of predictable stability. We safeguard this stability by passing the tradition of truth telling on to each generation. In all my years of studying history, anthropology, biographies, and international political science, I have never discovered evidence of a society of people who survived by encouraging deceitful behavior among its citizenship. Even sociopathic criminals have certain unwritten rules of honor they expect others to follow — "You can cheat and lie to everyone else, but never lie to me."

Although truth telling is a valued self-evident social construct, humans often violate this charge. Therefore, society finds it necessary to draft laws, codes, ordinances, declarations, and constitutions to outline the legal boundaries of acceptable public behavior. Theoretically, society grants freedom from punishment to those who obey established laws.

On an interpersonal level, we also create unofficial, but no less important, behavioral boundaries by giving someone the precious intangible gift of our promise. Written proclamations address formal promises made in a civic setting. Orally we make promises in the presence of public witnesses by taking oaths, pledges, vows, or by solemnly swearing. In sacred settings, we may make a covenant with our ethereal Creator.

Because I value truth telling I take these oaths, pledges, and vows very seriously. However, two words you will not hear me say are, "I promise." Although I did not begin the chapter with a story, let me pause here to share a brief personal account of why I do not promise anything to anyone.

When I was still a teenager, I made a critical promise to the father of my first serious girlfriend. Fate brought me to his hospital bedside just before he was about to go to surgery. I don't even recall what the surgery was for, but my impression was that it was not a life-threatening procedure. I was shocked and delighted that the family invited me into his hospital room along with other biological family members. After he had provided his children with hugs, kisses, and reassurances that everything would be all right, he looked over at me. I was standing in the shadows of the room's exit with my back pressed against the wall, attempting to be invisible. I had only come along to provide emotional support for my girlfriend. I wasn't part of the family. At that point in time, I still wasn't certain if he even wanted me dating his daughter. He spotted me and beckoned me with his hand, now adorned on the backside with an intravenous needle and tubing, to come over to the bed. He was a giant of a man who for no other reason than his eminent size frightened me. I thought to myself, *What could he possibly want to say to me?*

Maybe he wanted to tell me that I had no business being there with his family. Perhaps he just wanted to visually confirm I wasn't one of his children that he had inadvertently neglected to hug. Maybe he thought I was a delusion caused by the preoperative anesthesia I witnessed the nurse inject minutes prior into the IV port dangling in the back of his hand. I encouraged my reluctant feet to shuffle across eight to ten feet of linoleum floor to reach his bedside. He casually adjusted his IV-clad hand to engulf my relatively small trembling right hand in his.

With a sincere look of purpose from his sedation-induced weary brown eyes, he spoke to me in a low voice to say, "Take care of my daughter."

I recalled smiling slightly. I thought to myself, *Wow, maybe he actually likes me.* I then replied, "Yes, sir. I promise."

Later that evening, the receptionist at the surgical unit waiting room desk put down her phone and asked the family to assemble in the hospital chapel to speak with the surgeon. Once again, they invited me to join the family. At the time, I had no medical knowledge of value to add to the conversation. I had not even considered the prospect of going to medical school. However, since they invited me, I trailed the group into the little hospital chapel. I naively thought the chapel was where all families met surgeons after operations to discuss the outcome.

The surgeon arrived at the chapel about five to ten minutes after we sat down. His long white lab coat covered his wrinkled pale green surgical scrubs. I noticed his head hung low, intentionally not making any immediate eye contact with those present. He slowly removed his surgical cap prior to entering the conspicuously quiet room. He quietly closed the wood-framed door with stained-glass center, behind him. He looked about the room finding an acceptable seat among family members. I nervously stood near the only window in the room.

Something had gone wrong. Something had gone terribly wrong during the surgery. I could hear a concerned tone in his speech as he explained, in a voice just a hint above a whisper, the details of what had happened. I strained, with my limited medical knowledge, to understand what he was telling the family. Then the surgeon clearly announced, "We lost him." The next sound I heard were the echoes of wailing voices of sorrow careening off the tiny chapel's walls.

Over the next several years, I tried desperately to do as I had promised unknowingly to a dying man. However, acts of fate and destiny intervened to make it impossible for me to fulfill that promise. I lost touch with his daughter and all of her family members. From that day forth, I vowed never to promise anything to anyone if I did not have complete control over the outcome.

I continue the practice of never telling anyone, "I promise." I have found this to be an extremely liberating way to conduct my life. Those who know me well are aware of the fact I never promise anyone anything, but I make every effort to act is if I had. In the absence of "giving my word," I tend to overcompensate. I tend to fill the void with more than people expect and as if I had promised to do so.

When my daughters were still children, they would forget and utter the words, "Daddy, you promised…." Almost before the words left their mouth, they instantly knew my response would be, "I never promise anything."

"Dang," they would announce as they rolled their eyes and turned to stomp away.

Without telling anyone the detailed reason why I don't make promises, it has become a reassuring practice. It verifies whether my friends, family, coworkers, students, or patients are actively listening as I speak. If any of them attempt to rebuke me by saying, "You promised that you would…." I reply with complete certainty that they have misquoted me. I faithfully practice the doctrine of never making promises to do something that is beyond my full control to do. Very few things in life are immune to fate's intervention. Thus, very few things in life can be promised with certainty.

Let's conclude this chapter by circling back to the poem - *Unbelievable*.

Instead of attempting to digest the poem in one big bite, let's deconstruct it so we can eat away at its meaning by swallowing one portion of verse at a time.

Here I am,
    I'm unbelievable;
Invisible,
    I'm inconceivable.
Truth be told,
    No one here will care or ever notice;
Just stick to the plan,
using the status, they all are required to quote us.

Throughout life, there are circumstances and situations when we feel socially marginalized because of what we cherish, desire, or believe. We feel a palpable uneasiness when speaking in the presence of the cool kids or interacting with "normal" adults because we sense their discomfort in listening to our seemingly unorthodox points of view. Few want to be deemed as misfits or oddballs for deviating from the established social norm. This results in a seat alone in the corner of the lunchroom or the opportunity to be uninvited to the next big social event.

Truth telling, if it requires you to wander too far outside the socially accepted status quo, can deem you as unbelievable. The world continues to be flat if the majority of society wishes it to be so. Ridicule or banishment to the status of social invisibility awaits anyone who prematurely thinks differently.

That afternoon in the hospital, I desired the power to become invisible. As the only non-family member in the room, I felt uneasy being present at their patriarch's bedside. Somehow fate intervened to place me in an awkward, self-imposed situation where I made a promise I could not fulfill. The experience would subsequently change the way I conducted my life thereafter.

It still makes me cringe when I fail in my attempt to be an authentic truth teller — even if done in error. Have you ever given a stranger on the street directions only to realize after they left, you made a factual error? Many people would not give it a second thought. They will never see the stranger again. However, because of my bedside promise from years ago, I find that even small things, like providing the wrong directions, trouble me for the remainder of the day. I continue to wonder, more than is necessary, if the stranger ever arrived at their required destination. Did they think I gave the wrong directions intentionally? Why is caring about the truth so unbelievably exhausting? If only I could stick with the plan of caring less about the truth, it would be so much less troubling.

Yeah, look at me,
   I'm so unbelievable;
When I speak, I try to raise my voice,
   To drown out deceptions and give the believers an
   actual choice.

This second section of the poem demands we not hide our thoughts in the shadows of silence. It challenges us to do the contrary by raising our respective voices so other inconspicuous believers have the choice of being heard.

Throughout history, there have been courageous women and men who dared to reveal their unconventional beliefs to an unbelieving social community. In order to state their beliefs, some tendered their life as the ultimate sacrifice. Because of a covenant with God, scores of Jewish and later Christian faithful revealed their religious beliefs to ruling authorities risking the fate of a concentration camp inferno or the lion's den. Because they believed that forcefully keeping innocent humans in captured servitude was an unbelievable injustice, abolitionists risked their lives, lands, and fortunes to fight for an end to the institution of slavery in the United States. Because they desired a better life for people of all races, cultures, gender, and beliefs, thousands risked their lives and freedom by marching on hostile streets in search of cherished civil rights.

Instead of choosing to blend in invisibly with the status quo, the courageous must raise their collective voices in defiance of invalid social deceptions. When others in society witness these unbelievable acts of defiance, many more voices join the chorus of the truth tellers, demanding an end to visible injustices.

I speak few words hoping someone will hear a thing or two,

Wasting time creating broken rhymes about these changing times as if I have a clue;

These spoke words are seldom heard,

Because no bodies on earth are really listening to you.

Most of us have heard of the Gettysburg Address delivered by Abraham Lincoln on November 19, 1863. What is less well known is the somewhat astonishing fact that his historic speech only contained 272 words. There were other orators present at the Gettysburg battlefield dedication, but the soliloquies of their utterances have vanished in the depths of time. However, the awkward-appearing, self-educated log-splitter from Kentucky, who by an accident of fate become the president of the United States of America, caused all bodies present to remember all 272 words spoken in his three-minute message. His few words about the equality of men created equal in the eyes of their Creator profoundly inspired the masses. In dedicating the Gettysburg battlefield cemetery, he incorrectly lamented about a world who would not remember the few words he had spoken on that day. To the contrary, his few words have not since perished from the earth.

The verse sarcastically encourages us to keep doing and saying the right things even if no one is obviously listening. If what you believe is honorable, truthful, and is of value to all — be a persistent voice.

I want you to love my good, flaws, and ugly,

Because that's all a part of me;
Yeah, I'm so unbelievable
But that's what I strive to be.

This middle section of the poem asks us to pause for a moment to hold a mirror up to ourselves. There we will see various reflections of the evolving creation we are striving to become. Despite our desire to always be good citizens of the earth, we inevitability stumble on life's torrential path. Fate and failure are brutal educators about our existing imperfections. Both expose our less than desirable human flaws. It is an unbelievable pretense to think we are capable of being faultless. Historically, those seeking to silence the truth tellers expose the human character flaws of the messenger. This mockery is always the first defense of those who wish to maintain the social status quo. Their hope is to nullify the messenger's unbelievable thoughts by pointing out the fact that she/he is not perfect—and thus not to be taken seriously. Do not be fearful of these feeble assaults because the prevailing truth will vanquish their attempts to silence you. Continue to be a persistent voice of reason.

Attempt to maximize the good in your life. Minimize the less than desirable human traits, while realizing our defects also have purpose. Some flaws, by necessity, must remain to preserve our unique human nature. When I was a child, I noticed my mother had a scar on the left cheek of her face. It was about the size of a US quarter and almost looked like a silhouette of the state of Ohio. I never gave it a second thought until I saw a map of Ohio hanging on my grade school wall. It prompted me one day to ask my mother, "How did you get that mark on your face?" She shared the story of how, when she was a very small child, she was sitting in a rocking chair by an open fireplace. The chair tipped casting her into the open flames. Badly burned, she has scars on the small area on her face and her left arm. While telling me the story, she showed me the scars on her left forearm. She had those scars my entire life. They resided on her face and on one of those two arms that so frequently hugged me, yet I had never consciously noticed them. When I did finally notice, I never thought to ask about their origin, at least not until I had reached elementary school age. I just always thought of my mommy as beautiful. I was blind to the visible deformity on her cheek. It was never an obvious distraction from her physical or spiritual beauty. I simply saw her as flawless and loved every aspect of her existence.

This section of the poem speaks to us about how God grants us the ability to see beyond human imperfections to find the true essence of love. True love isn't based on the shallowness of physical attraction, the desire of social status, or the want of sexual pleasure. A grander force unconditionally consecrates true love for another human being. This attraction brings separate spirits together to create one similar consciousness. Because of their desire to dwell as one, they are not fearful of allowing the other to view the chronicles of their good, flawed, and ugly life reflections. The aggregate of their separate life experiences becomes the mortar binding them together in love. To truly love someone is to joyfully accept every part of them regardless of the acknowledged imperfections. The enduring spiritual strength of true love completes a vital human need. It promotes our determination to become a more, impeccable mortal creation. Love faithfully whispers to our souls that it will not abandon us during our journey toward a fulfilled life on earth.

> **I tell them facts to see how they will react,**
> **I've been told that facts don't ever lie;**
> **We've all been told truth is good for something,**
> **But there are those out there who ask me why.**

In the previous chapter, we discussed how to arrive at wisdom by going through the linear progression of **awareness, education, knowledge, and truth**. This verse asks why we react so negatively to evidence-based facts, as if they were pure fiction, when they fail to fit into the view of the world we elect to believe. Historically, this is a human character trait. In literature, oceans of ink depict how certain historic figures have denied mountains of objective evidence placed before them to arrive at critically wrong decisions. Countless millions of lives, careers, relationships, positions of leadership, wars, and countries have been lost because of someone's desire to believe the unbelievable instead of the existing facts.

This verse puzzles as to why there are so many people who say facts don't matter. Despite acknowledging our preference to exist in a society where truth is a preprogrammed expectation, a distressing number of individuals remain convinced that modern society can successfully function using indiscriminate versions of near facts, shifting truths, and unverified beliefs.

Truth is the gold standard of measurement we must always use if we are preparing for a somewhat predictable future. Aspirational beliefs of what we want the future to be, not what it can become, contaminate wishful facts.

I'm right here for you,
   I'm unbelievable;
      My presence here is not so unconceivable.
My momma told me, "boy you should never lie."
But when I speak the truth you never cease to ask me why.

The next to the last section of the poem practically screams to the reader to recognize the truth when it reveals itself. "I'm right here for you." Can't you see me?

It is peculiar how the truth clings to us despite our best attempts to ignore it. I mentioned earlier how despondent I become when I give someone the wrong directions. It nags me long after the mistake occurs. To my knowledge, other than someone getting lost, erroneous directions have never resulted in an immediate loss of life. However, as a Doctor of Medicine, it is my duty always to enlist confirmed facts to make correct decisions. Trust is the quintessential element of the medical profession. The Hippocratic Oath compels physicians to "do no harm." Attempting to do the right thing at all times is critical to patients who are literally entrusting the care of their lives to me. In my vocation, I must commit to a career of life-long learning and seek verifiable information to cure disease. My personal beliefs in non-proven medical folklore have no valid role to play in my care of patients. You would not want to entrust your life to an airline pilot who successfully lands the plane without crashing 90 percent of the time nor would you trust your life to a doctor who, on average, accidentally kills a patient one or two times a year.

Ironically, even with all of the years of medical training a physician has to endure and the numerous hours of experiential knowledge we accumulate during our clinical practice, some patients prefer to believe in unbelievable cures they see in print, on social media, or hear about from a friend or relative with no medical background. It is inconceivable why this happens. Perhaps there is something innate in our human psychosocial DNA, enticing us to believe the unbelievable, especially when it comes to magical medical cures.

The truth is not always recognized by the eyes of those who blindly receive it,

Is it so overwhelming we can never comprehend, check it out, or dare to believe it?

Here I am I'm not so invisible;

Here I am — I promise — I'm not unbelievable.

The poem concludes by challenging the reader to open his/her eyes to see the truth surrounding them. It's not invisible. Sometimes it's so boldly displayed before us we cannot recognize it for what it is.

It asks us to strive constantly for improvements in life. The path of truth is a journey worth taking. Don't heed the temptation to look for detours, shortcuts, or off-ramps. There will be patches of rough road making navigation difficult. Fate's potholes will unexpectedly appear to challenge you. These unforeseen occurrences will knock you off your stride. They may even trip you up and bring you to your knees. I have been there. Take the opportunity while you are down there on the ground to say a prayer before you rise up to take your next steps forward. Always march forward. Proceed with the truth clearly in mind. You can never find the future by looking for it in the past.

As you rise up, look to see if someone else is there taking a similar journey. If they extend a welcoming hand to join them, consider taking it — especially if they "promise" to do you no harm.

Oh, by the way, I recently found social media correspondence from my teenage girlfriend whose story I told earlier in this chapter. She is living happily with someone she dearly loves and has earned her doctoral degree. When I saw this post, I smiled at the image emitting from my computer screen. I sat back in my chair and breathed a soulful sigh of relief. She seems to have done well. Perhaps my limited presence in her life was enough to alter its trajectory in a positive direction after all. Perhaps it would have proceeded the way it did regardless of my presence. I would like to think I did something of significance to fulfill the ill-fated promise I made when I was nineteen years old. Maybe, just maybe, it was not my purpose always to be there to ensure her happiness. Perhaps, as promised, my purpose was to remain a caring fixture in her life just long enough to nudge it toward a path of enduring joy.

Destiny and fate will always offer us opportunities to change the status quo.

Reality (truth) is the absolute zero of life — unachievable, but always worth seeking.

CHAPTER NINE

"We need to teach our youth to become men and women of great character and how not to simply grow up to be characters."

When I was a child, I spent a great deal of time lying on my belly just a few feet from the large walnut console RCA television in our living room. Situated by the staircase adjacent to the front door entrance, it was our most noticeable piece of furniture to any arriving visitor. The black and white images emitting from behind that television's glass screen became my window into a world of possibilities. My vivid imagination always served to supplement my limited childhood understanding of destinations beyond the reach of a local bus or cab. The fantasies spurred by looking at picture books and magazines, listening to the little tan Zenith radio on our mantel and the black 78 rpm records my mother bought me at the local Goodwill store, and watching the mesmerizing images produced by the RCA console far exceeded anything my imagination alone could conjure.

Like most children of my era, I enjoyed Saturday morning television programming. During the 1960s through the 1980s, I was one of the approximately twenty million children in the United States visually glued to the television screen on Saturday morning watching shows and commercials that introduced us to the next must-have toys. It was five solid hours of cartoon delight! I would roll on the floor laughing until my gut ached as I watched the Looney Tunes characters devise creative ways to blow each other up and drop enormous objects on one another. Although these cartoon scenes were unquestionably violent by today's standard, I never knew any kids who didn't understand that cartoons were only make believe. It wasn't until live-action shows were introduced to the children's television lineup that I witnessed kids in my neighborhood, mostly boys, trying to emulate their favorite hero or villain by kicking the living daylight out of one another.

Children's television is nearly as old as the invention of commercial TV itself. In 1928, WRGB, in Schenectady, New York, became the world's first television station. By 1946, only 0.5 percent of US households had a television. The legendary children's puppet program, *Kukla, Fran and Ollie*, aired on television in 1947. As a kid, I remember seeing reruns of this program, wondering how kids of that era spent their mornings watching sock puppets pretend to talk. It was obvious to me that there was a guy behind the box talking. With that said, I am certain children today would find the children's shows I enjoyed when I was a kid stupidly boring.

As the number of television sets in US households grew, so did the number of children's programs and commercial advertisements. Parents quickly noted the enormous impact television had on children. In 1952, the first panel on violence and children's television convened to address the commercialization of kid's entertainment. However, it was not until 1969 that the Public Broadcasting Station (PBS) show *Sesame Street* became the first commercial-free children's TV program. A decade later the US Congress enacted the Children's Television Act to garner greater parental involvement in network programming decisions; provide more educational content in programs; decrease the amount of violence seen on TV; and lessen the stereotypical racial and gender biases previously displayed in children's television media.

By 1990, the number of children watching traditional commercial TV had dropped to around two million. Morning news and teen or adult entertainment features supplanted Saturday morning children's programming. Over the ensuing decades, children had the option of watching cable networks, videocassette recorder (VCR) tapes, digital video discs (DVD), and digitally accessed media programs designed specifically for them.

Through the screen of our television set, I watched cartoons, cowboys, clowns, cops and robbers, comedies, and heroes. Watching TV led me to draw my own conclusions about the vast world I had yet to discover. Supplemented by the value systems my adult guardians granted me, I learned how to recognize society's stereotypical definitions of good people and bad people by watching TV. The villains always wore black and the heroes wore white. The evildoers never smiled like the toothy-grin, good guys. The bad dudes were usually fairly dumb, spoke poor English, and/or had darker skin than their heroic counterparts.

As a child, I never wondered why so few ethnic or "colored" characters appeared in the children's movies or cartoons I watched on TV. While it was not important to me as a five-year-old, the stereotypes undoubtedly imprinted a subliminal message on my developing subconscious brain. The first black characters I vaguely recall seeing on TV were a comedy duo named Amos and Andy. Although they were hilarious in their depictions of urban life, they did not remind me of any colored families I knew. From my vantage point as a preschool child, I thought when I saw actors on TV that I was looking at scenes of people who were real. Cartoon characters, on the other hand, were make believe.

I eventually realized a significant number of non-minority adults viewing these shows had a slightly similar impression. Some see early television shows depicting ethnic groups in stereotypical roles as a genuine twentieth century equivalent to our twenty-first-century network "reality shows," only with a laugh track. Unfortunately, a significant number of Americans continue to view the exploits seen on today's "reality shows" (which production experts have appropriately edited to give the appearance of being actual reality) as emblematic of certain acceptable lifestyles. These factitious episodes validate stereotypes of how certain people, rich or poor, conduct themselves in society.

As I grew older, I realized that I was not actually looking into the homes of real people through the lens of our TV. These were actors playing roles to demonstrate how most good, God fearing, "normal people" live their lives in America. Lying prone with my head propped up on a pillow in the middle of the living room floor, I saw the characters on TV residing in beautiful homes, driving long, luxurious cars, living the American dream. The limited minorities I saw on TV in the 1960s fell into a few broad stereotypical categories. Asians were mysterious and devious. Colored people and Africans were domestics (i.e. maids and butlers), childlike background characters, overweight, and obedient. Mexicans were lazy gunslinging desperados. Eastern Indians were manservants, safari guides, or mystical genies. Native American Indians were always trying to steal the cowboy's land.

Despite seldom seeing anyone like me on television, I internalized qualities I most admired in each television or movie character. I wanted to be someone's hero. I was particularly attracted to the TV character Superman. Not only was he invincible, he had super strength, could run faster than a speeding bullet, could see through solid walls, and he could fly. Superman stood for truth, justice, and the American way. I decided at an early age that I wanted to grow up to be Superman.

I was the little kid running around the backyard with a cape, (towel) tied around my neck. After having gotten to the apex of my capability on the Riverview Park swing set, I would close my eyes and lean back to enjoy the sensation of gravity pulling me back to earth causing the wind to whistle by my ears. My imagination told me this is what it must feel like to fly at super speed. At some point when no adults were watching, I would summon the courage to jump off the swing at the apex of its forward pitch to see how far I could fly. I was extremely fortunate to have never injured myself during these attempts to defy gravity, but for a brief moment, I always had the hope of discovering my hidden super power of flight.

As I grew older, I realized my career aspirations of becoming a superhero, without any detectable super powers, were limited. However, I did acquire the ability to read. At some point in my young life, I discovered comic books. Thrilled to learn that my hero Superman had his own comic book, I used money earned from my paper route to buy comic books each week. Throughout most of my adolescent years, I followed the life and adventures of superheroes by reading comic books. My ferocious appetite for reading comic books greatly improved my vocabulary. I recall my third-grade teacher, Mrs. Hensley, being perplexed at how I knew certain words uncharacteristic of a child my age. These comic books also piqued my interest in science and social politics, and ignited my interest in reading about actual flesh and blood social heroes.

With time, I became increasingly interested in world history. I loved to read about historical figures, who without benefit of superhuman powers, became catalysts in igniting historic social change in the era in which they lived.

During my teenage years, I began listening attentively to the sweet medleys of the music coming out of the radio perched on our living room fireplace mantel. I listened to the meaning of the poetic lyrics written by the urban music philosophers from the 1960s and '70s. I tried to imagine the situations or circumstances the songwriter must have personally encountered to motivate the songs of love, social struggle, coming of age, hope, revolution, and the dawning of a better future. A chosen few of these artists had special superpowers that allowed them to create and perform songs to inspire. The rhythm of their music opened young minds to the possibility of becoming better than the stereotypical norms propagated by previous generations. My classmates elected to sing some of those songs of hope at our eighth-grade graduation. As we marched off the stage at Longfellow Elementary, I resigned myself to the fact that I would never defy Earth's physical gravity, but, at the very least, I could become a social hero of sort by defying the gravity of low expectations.

We need to teach our youth to become men and women of great character and how not to simply grow up to be characters.

One afternoon at work, I recall having a conversation with one of my coworkers. During our casual discussion, I mentioned that I grew up in Dayton, Ohio. This heightened her attention because she too had grown up in Dayton.

She asked, "What elementary school did you attend?"

I replied, "Longfellow Elementary."

She immediately displayed a puzzled look. After a brief moment of bewildered silence, she exclaimed, "I thought that was a school for gifted children."

I didn't miss a beat in replying, "So, what's your point?" Our conversation screeched to an abrupt halt as she examined the smug little grin, I intentionally arranged on my face. I knew she was thinking that this guy doesn't look or act like a genius. I apparently did not conform to her stereotypical image of a genius. I have no idea where she got her notion of what a Longfellow alum was supposed to look like. I could only guess that a skinny six-foot tall African American male did not fit her expectations. I broke the silence by stating, "Well, it wasn't for gifted kids when I went there." I forced a laugh and moved on to another topic of conversation.

Upon further reflection, I began to wonder what variables contribute to our intuitive expectations. Humans routinely use stereotypical defaults to prejudge others based solely on an individual's visible external characteristics. Each day we use our rapid intuitive reasoning and, if necessary, our slower deductive reasoning, to mentally evaluate individuals we encounter. I may see a friend at the end of the day, slouched in a chair, and conclude it was an exhausting day at work for him. I may also see an impeccably dressed stranger walk by on the street and conclude she is intellectually gifted and/or wealthy.

Both observations, without the use of my slower deductive reasoning capabilities to further examine the situation, might be in error. As I recall, my friend has always had poor posture. When I asked about his day, he indicated he skipped work to spend the day at the beach. Overall, it was a relaxing day. The stranger on the street borrowed a nice outfit from her girlfriend's closet to go to a job interview. She had been couch surfing with friends since losing her job and apartment four months ago. In both cases, my intuition failed to conform with reality.

Often, examining superficial human characteristics predicates our perspective on what to expect. Social preprogramming alerts our biological fight or flight impulses. These impulses are strengthened by survival instructions provided to us by our parents or guardians, our personal life experiences, virtual input from social media, or even by an epiphany of spiritual origin. In previous chapters, we discussed some of these preprogrammed influences, so let's focus our attention on the impact of mass media.

Mass media has grown exponentially since 1952 when the first Panel on Violence and Children's Television convened. Even during the dawn of television programming for children, parent groups expressed their collective concerns about how the presence of television in the household could adversely affect the social development of children. Television has its merits and its demons. Educational programming can increase the vocabulary and intellectual growth of both children and adults. It can also induce the viewer to see a world beyond their closed social environment. This provides the viewer with an opportunity to appreciate the variability of human conditions different from their own.

Media exposure to violence on television and video games, in social media, and at the movies is the subliminal demon lurking on screen that can desensitize the viewer to the value of a human life. A child exposed to such violence may become either fearful or clueless of genuine danger existing in the world around them. As I observed with my childhood colleagues who watched generous amounts of violence on TV and at the movies, many became more aggressive in their play as they attempted to duplicate the stunts done by their favorite action heroes. While my failed attempt to fly from the swing fortunately failed to result in injury, an unfortunate few of my childhood friends did suffer serious injury. One actually died while attempting to jump from one rooftop to another.

Adults are not immune to the demons of mass media. They can become fearful of adverse social outcomes. They may polarize themselves from certain groups of people because they choose to bathe themselves in a homogenous, opinion-focused media source. In the battle for ratings, the lines between reality and reality television entertainment blur by intent. Parents should offer their children a variety of educational mediums. Limiting daily screen time for children should not be a form of punishment.

Just as it is customary for a parent to sit at the dinner table with their child to ensure they consume appropriate nutrients, it should be equally important for the parent to participate in screen time activities with the child. Take this time to answer the questions a curious child may have about consumed media content. Seek out opportunities for these conversations with our children—don't shun them.

As children come of age, they have an innate desire to discover the world on their own terms. Our parents and guardians provided us with the basic essentials for understanding the laws, social norms, and cultural traditions we require to survive the transition to adulthood. Our parents become the voice of our moral consciousness by providing us with their definitions of right and wrong. They were the initial little voice in our head speaking to us when we were about to do something wrong.

During our adolescence years, we begin to witness inconsistencies in what our guardians taught us. This inconsistency between these teachings and the reality of what grown-ups actually do begins to concern us more during our teenage years. This results in what some call "teenage rebellion." Just as we did as toddlers, the teenager ventures out of her/his established zone of social comfort to begin a process of self-verification. When established social dogma is inconsistent with what the teen has discovered through the process of self-verification, the youth may challenge their parent or guardian to prove the rule's validity.

We have dominion over our children for a relatively short span of time during their biological existence on this earth. Therefore, it is our duty to use this time wisely. The imprinting of a child's fundamental personality characteristics occurs in the first decade of a child's life. The concept of role modeling for our children is vitally important before age ten. This tipping point in their young life is where the child begins to discover life outside their immediate family unit. Their world begins expanding rapidly to include new friends and acquaintances who may not be as familiar with the child's household norms. They begin to realize that not everyone in their newly discovered world lives in a manner consistent with their family unit. There are people who speak different languages, think differently, play differently, pray differently, have different definitions of a family unit, and have varying beliefs regarding the world in which we all reside.

Recognizing that these life transitions would eventually happen to my children, I decided to forewarn them of this inevitability in a somewhat novel way. I don't know where I came up with the idea, but while my two daughters were still less than ten years old, I decided to begin having character-building conversations with each of them as they reached certain milestone ages. Even though I am a family physician, I left the menstrual cycle talk at age ten to their mother. The conversation regarding religious choice occurred at age twelve. At age thirteen, I took each of them on their first official date.

Conversations about the importance of a college education, driving, dating, and permission to get ears pierced occurred at age sixteen. There was not a conversation about body tattoos other than they could not have one until after their eighteenth birthday. You guessed it. I took each of them to get their driving permits and their ears pierced on their sixteenth birthday. They each got a tattoo when they were eighteen—go figure.

Although I did not do so with prescriptive intention, we laid the groundwork for future "conversations" by providing our children with character-building guidelines to follow prior to having the formal discussions about why these experiences were essential. As an example, prior to having the conversation about religious choice at age twelve, our children attended church on a regular basis. As they grew older, they began to ask questions about the sermons, rituals, and the songs sung. During our conversations about religion, we told both that it was up to them to seek God based on their own personal experiences and not that of their parents. Our job was to make them aware of how to approach achieving spiritual wisdom in their life. It was not to make our children select a particular religious philosophy prior to them understanding the significance of their action. I still remember seeing my youngest daughter, Ciara, spontaneously tearing up after a sermon one Sunday morning. Without my prompting, she left her seat beside me and approached the altar to accept Jesus Christ as her Lord and personal savior. I smiled and said a silent prayer of gratitude. Baptized at age twelve, Ciara had arrived at this choice by taking her own spiritual journey—not because I demanded it.

At age thirteen, I took each of my daughters on their first official date. We both dressed up in nice outfits. I selected a fashionable restaurant for dinner. From the very beginning of the dinner date, I explained how a real gentleman, one who truly cared about them, should treat them on a date. As they had always seen me do for their mother, I opened the car door for them. I opened the door to the restaurant for them. I pulled out their chair at the table. During dinner, we talked about the perilous journey they were about to begin as teenagers. I shared with them the fact that the IQ of their parents would seem to plummet to single digits as they progressed through their teenage years. During their teens, the perception of their personal IQ would subjectively go high into triple digits — as it pertained to how the world should operate. Of course, the parents' IQ would somehow miraculous rebound back to normal by the time their teenage years are past. Each of them laughed out loud at my description. Eventually, the conversation turned to relationships, boyfriends, and the true meaning of being in love. I encouraged them to ask me any questions about the inconsistencies in life they were now observing.

At the end of our date, my comment to each of them went something like this, "From the moment you were born, and I first looked into your eyes, I knew you would never need us more than you needed us on the day of your birth. I immediately fell in love with you, but I've had to let you go just a tiny bit each day since you were born as you began to discover a vast new world around you. That world consists of people other than your mother and me. I know the day will come when I will have to let you go on to live your life independent of us. But as long as I exist on this earth remember I will always be there for you." It was difficult to get those words out on both occasions. Our date would end by me giving them each a small golden ring for them to wear engraved with the words, "True love waits." As each found their true loves, wedding rings replaced the rings I presented to them when they were thirteen.

I informed each of them at their first date that attending college was non-negotiable—they were going. Education is a self-created super power each of them was required to embrace. An education is an invaluable asset to avoid future traps of dependence on someone other than themselves for financial support. After completing college, I pledged to take each daughter on a trip to a location of their choice so we could have our first official father-adult daughter conversation. It was also my opportunity to verify to them that my IQ had returned to normal.

In this age of 24/7 news cycles and being constantly plugged into data, some young people have difficulty hearing wisdom through all the background noise. They struggle to take notice of how to develop their own unique character. Even mature adults have increasing difficulty in successfully shaking off the constant media intrusions that invade our daily lives. Many of our youth, and even adults, see "characters" in the media and simply attempt to be like them. It may be hip to dress like the rock star you admire, but it does not provide you with the strength of character to value the pursuit of truth. Seeking acceptance by sharing the political views of peers will not inspire you to value justice for all people regardless of their opposing political perspective. Becoming a "character" who does outrageous acts in public to garner attention may make people notice you for the moment, but it will be the unnoticed courageous acts you do that will make you a person of great character.

As we venture out into a world of our own making, we need to take time to have substantial conversations with as many people of interest as we possibly can. Experience life's inconsistencies and learn how to reconcile them with joy by marching forward toward truth not hearsay. Jumping from childhood to adulthood (or off the swing at its highest apex) can be a perilous vault if you do so expecting to fly like a superhero. First, you need the impregnable chains of a well-developed character to defy the gravity of a fall from social grace.

After arriving at adulthood, we must resist the gravitational pulls of falsehoods, hatred, and injustices by exhibiting the strength of character to do the right thing instead of just acting like a character produced for the purpose of entertainment in a falsely simulated reality. Be a consistent role model for others. Do not allow the young people you mentor or influence to grow up with an ambition to imitate social characters. Teach them instead to be persons of great character.

When I reflect back to that child lying on his living room floor watching *Superman* on television, I now realize why Superman's creators (Jerry Siegel and Joe Shuster) gave him a secret identity. I used to wonder why he didn't want to be Superman all of the time. Being a full-time hero is challenging. When the world sees you as an invincible (perfect) individual, they assume you are also emotionally invincible. Superman's alter ego, the mild-mannered Clark Kent from rural Kansas, was able to reveal his human emotions and imperfections. As Mr. Kent, he could be like everyone else around him. People loved him as an ordinary human being, not because he had super powers (i.e. extreme wealth, fame, political influence, a position at the apex of the social hierarchy, etc.). The biographical histories of recognized social heroes often reveal a less than perfect life journey. Many fear the ever-present specter of failure and the loneliness of lacking love for reasons other than their social position. Even superheroes need the time to relax, experience love, and just be human.

During conversations with the young people in your life, encourage them to become women and men of great character, but do not demand they achieve perfection. Instead, teach your children to be loving human beings to all. Emphasize the undeniable fact that, because they originated from your essence, your love for them is unconditional. Don't predicate love on the child's ability to follow the "perfect life" we have prescribed for them.

The want of perfection is the kryptonite that can weaken or even vanquish the spirit of those who have the strongest convictions to be full-time heroes and she-roes. Our Creator loves us not because we are perfect, but because we are His most-perfect creation.

"Change" is like an ever-present life partner who I despise when it takes me from my comfort zone, but love when it reveals my potential to become a better person.

CHAPTER TEN

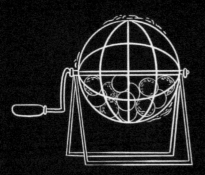

"Fate has its virtue."

In this book's introduction, I explained how I randomly selected the ten quotes for each chapter by putting a copy of each quote into a kitchen cookie jar — similar to the one that sat on the top of my mother's refrigerator for most of my entire childhood. I pulled each slip of paper, containing a quote, out of the jar to determine which ten (there were about eighty quotes in the jar) to use as chapter themes. I wrote each chapter in the sequence I drew quotes from the jar. During the process of reading the emerging pieces of paper, I was tempted to change the order of the ten quotes or to repeat the exercise until I got an arrangement of quotes I preferred. I did neither. If fate was truly going to assist me in the construction of this project, something told me I should not interfere. When I looked at the quote typed on the final folded slip of paper, the four words staring back at me were "**Fate has its virtue.**" Lesson learned. It seemed appropriate to conclude the final chapter of this little book with my oldest and briefest uttering from the edge of nowhere.

I spent nine of my first thirteen years of life roaming the echoing halls of Longfellow Elementary School. I left the mammoth red brick building with the ornate gray slate roof for the last time after my eighth-grade graduation ceremony concluded. Constructed in 1860, the original building (called the 11th District School) inherited the name Longfellow School upon completion of its two additions in 1950. With the exclusion of my cousins who lived on the other side of Dayton, practically every kid I knew up to that point in my life attended Longfellow Elementary. On Longfellow's black asphalt playground, I learned what I thought were all of the essential secrets of life. From kindergarten through eighth grade, I learned the alphabet and how to tie my shoes; write my name in cursive; recite the pledge of allegiance; play well with others; shoot marbles and win; and hang upside down from the top rung of the boys' monkey bars without falling. I figured out that girls were actually "kind of" interesting to be around; that life is not always fair; that even kids can die; and bullies are scary. And, oh yeah, I also learned about arithmetic, science, and social studies. Without a doubt, the best thing I learned was how to read chapter books that did not have pictures in them.

After my eighth-grade graduation ceremony, my mother and I began our walk through the neighborhood back home. As we were waiting for the light to change at the crosswalk just outside the school building, I looked back and pointed up at the new large white and green plywood sign hanging from the black iron fire escape on the side of the Longfellow school building. At the end of the school year, students made the sign in shop class. Reportedly, people, unfamiliar with the ancient building on Salem Avenue, did not know it was a school. So students participated in a contest to come up with a slogan and a sign to place on the side of the building to identify it. I proudly told my mother how our art teacher selected me to help paint the plywood sign white and fill in the large green letters she had outlined with the slogan: **This is Longfellow where we try harder to make school better.** It hung on that fire escape for nearly twenty years, before weathering forced its removal. As a young adult, every time I drove by Longfellow, I would look up at my sign. It reminded me of all those wonderful and whimsical years of life I spent within that grand old building. It also reminded me of friends who left my life.

I still vividly recall one particular summer evening after our eighth-grade graduation, but before the beginning of high school. We had the summer free to do whatever our young hearts desired. We were officially teenagers! At our graduation, we sang songs of hope and gave speeches about how we would someday make the world a better place for future generations. We knew we had all the answers to life's puzzling questions. We would certainly get around to solving these problems once we completed the process of growing up and having fun.

Every summer my best friend, James, and his siblings would go to East St. Louis to stay with their father. They returned to Dayton prior to the beginning of the new school year. On the day of James's scheduled return, I scampered over to James's house to welcome him back home and catch up on "stuff." James and I lived one small city block (about half the length of a football field) away from each other. A block long section of asphalt-paved alley separated the backyard of his house from the front yard of mine. Traveling east from James's backyard, the section of the alley merged onto Williams Street in front of my house. In the winter, when the tree foliage was absent, I could stand on my porch and see the outer edge of James's backyard, precisely the spot where they placed their large metal garbage cans at the alley's edge for pickup on trash day.

I was somewhat surprised to see James sitting on a large rock at the alley's edge talking to two other boys I didn't know. James was a handsome youth. His skin was the color of the light caramel we dipped apples in. His sandy brown curly Afro had grown noticeably in length during his hiatus from Dayton. James had what my mother classified as "good hair." I guessed that meant what I was growing on top of my head was "bad hair." Along with our hair, both of us had also grown in height during our summer absence from each other. But, this particular summer James had grown in more ways than height. I detected some facial hair emerging from above his upper lip.

He was back in Dayton with a new hairdo, more vertical height, facial hair, and new friends. Other than maybe being a half inch taller, I was still the same skinny kid with bad hair who had graduated from Longfellow Elementary in early June. James introduced me to the other two guys. To this day, I do not recall their names. I don't remember what they looked like. I just stood silently with my head down pretending to be interested in kicking rocks around in the dirt while they continued with their conversation. I desperately wished the two strangers would leave so I could talk to James about the stuff best friends like us talk about. Nothing the three of them were discussing seemed relevant to me. I suddenly felt a flash of fear that I had not only lost my best friend for the summer, but that James was about replace me with a more mature group of guy friends who could talk about things real teenagers valued. Maybe they had all come of age during the summer while I was languishing both physically and emotionally in an extended childhood.

While I listened for opportunities to provide comments to the conversation, I glanced over at James. He was still sitting on the large rock now with a stick in his hand, writing something in the dirt as he listened to the other two boys' banter. He was preoccupied with whatever words or artwork he was creating in the dirt when a stray black dog came up to him. The dog positioned itself over whatever James had been scribbling in the dirt. James began to pet the dog and talking doggy to it. That was the James I knew and loved. I knew he was in there somewhere. Maybe he was just hanging out with these guys to be cool.

The summer days were longer than at any time of the year, but the sun had begun to drop beneath the horizon enough to cause the white glow of the alley's street light to become noticeable. To this day, I still do not know why, but I suddenly experienced an overwhelming sense of fatigue. Both the emerging evening darkness and exhaustion seemed to blanket me simultaneously. James was still playing with the dog while the other two boys remained absorbed in their own conversation about a topic foreign to me. I told James and the others goodbye. During the introductions, I learned that the two other boys lived about a block east of my house. Since school hadn't started back yet, I normally would have just hung out with James until late in the evening. But tonight, I seemed to be the odd man out in the group, so I took the opportunity to go home and get in bed early. Perhaps my exhaustion was less physical and more emotional due to my sad thoughts of potentially losing my best friend forever.

I slowly walked back through the alley toward home. With bowed head, I watched each of my steps, thinking about what I had experienced. Why didn't I grow up as much as James did that summer? Who was going to be my best friend if James didn't want to be my friend anymore? Halfway home, the alley light on the post revealed a few large interesting rocks I could kick along the way as I thought about James. When I got home, I immediately went upstairs to my bedroom. I quickly peeled off my clothes and got in bed. Sleep captured me instantaneously.

Deep in sleep, I was stunned to near consciousness by what sounded like a canon firing. A second booming sound rattled the windows of the house and several loose objects in my room. Then I heard tires squealing in the distance followed by a car rapidly accelerating south on Williams Street toward my house. The sound of the car quickly faded into the quiet of the night. I felt my heart racing, but I did not get out of bed to inquire about the sequence of unusual sounds emanating from outside. Within seconds, my unrelenting need for sleep recaptured me. I did not recall hearing any other awakening sounds for the remainder of the night.

The next morning, I went downstairs to the kitchen and saw my mother sitting at the table drinking a cup of coffee and watching the morning news on our portable television. The television news reporter described a fatal drive-by shooting that had occurred in Dayton last night. The suspect randomly shot two boys from his car at the corner of Williams and Holt Street. One boy died from his wounds. As I was absorbing the news from the television, I realized that the canon blasts I thought were a dream were actually the sound of a shotgun firing. I looked at my mother's sadly concerned face. I had never seen her cry about anything, but her eyes revealed evidence of prior tears. She struggled to explain to me how James was the fatally wounded victim in the incident reported on TV.

Everything else that day was a mental blur. I just kept remembering the last hour I spent with James. He seemed so at peace with his young life. Even the little black dog who approached him in the alley selected James that night providing him with a moment of loving attention. The events of the fateful evening replayed in my head all day long. If the other two boys hadn't been there, I wouldn't have decided to go home early. James and I would have been the ones under the streetlight when the stranger with the shotgun drove by looking for young black males to shoot. [Author's Note: Years later, authorities apprehended the deranged killer as he attempted to gain entry to a federal court building with the intent of murdering a federal judge. The man was angry about the legal enforcement of federally mandated school busing in the city. The series of shots were his method of protesting the court orders]. If fate had not stricken me with a sudden overwhelming sense of fatigue, I probably would have walked home with James and the two other boys to the corner of Holt and Williams Street, instead of detouring through the alley. We had few fears back then. Most likely, the boys continued their conversation as James walked the other boys back home when the man with the shotgun spotted them. When I left James for the last time that evening, fearing I was about to lose my best friend, I did not realize how prophetic my unshakable fear had been. I never imagined how swiftly and tragically I would permanently lose my best friend. Had I not been safe in bed sleeping at that fateful hour, my mother might have been sitting alone at our kitchen table that morning watching reports about the death of her son and his best friend, James. I think she would have cried.

As children, James and I shared mountains of comic books, played cowboys and Indians, cops and robbers, pretended to be heroic soldiers, master spies, and superheroes. We could talk about anything without fear of reprisal. We were going to go on to enjoy high school together. We were going to save the world together. We were going to be best friends forever — but fate intervened to change all of our most hopeful dreams.

"Fate has its virtue"

As I pondered the origins of these quotes, I was amazed that the ten chosen for each chapter of this book somehow flowed together in a logical fashion. When I initially stood at my kitchen counter looking at the slips of paper I had sequentially pulled from the cookie jar, I did not see how each chapter could possibly transition into the next in a meaningful way. Each quote seemed so random. Each quote arrived at random periods of my life, often separated by decades of life experiences. As I read this last slip of paper with the quote, "Fate has its virtue" I realized it was the first quote I took the notion to write down nearly thirty years ago. Prior to that time, I simply carried them around in my thoughts.

Given the perplexing task of someday weaving this random sequence of quotes into a book, I initially considered either reorganizing the quotes into a more desired chronology or, better still, just going through the quotes to select the quotes I felt most comfortable writing about. Life got in the way, causing me to put the project away for over a year. Another life event caused me to remember the content of the cookie jar sitting atop my refrigerator. Fate brought me back to the ten little slips of paper with the quotes written on them. After a year's absence from the project, something inside me had certainly changed or evolved. I suddenly realized how life's events are like the sequence of those ten little quotes. Each quote was a reverberation of wisdom acquired from an earlier salient life experience. With time, each quote assisted me in achieving better understanding of the complex world of human events surrounding me. Thus, I resisted the temptation to reorder the chapters. I simply began to write each chapter when inspired to do so in the sequence fate had intended. If someone read the book in a different sequence, hopefully, the virtue of fate would provide an appropriate narrative meaning to the reader.

Our lives are akin to an intentional novel created every day about our existence here on Earth. It begins with our introduction at birth. Our parents, having written multiple chapters of their own life's book, provide us with the basic table of contents we need to learn how to begin our life novel. At some point early in our existence, our trusted guardian(s) preemptively prepare our book with pages of their desired life outcomes for us based on their dreams and expectations. Yes, once upon a time those who loved us most wished us only to live a life of "happily ever after."

Our guardians' prescribed sections of our life book would follow this basic sequence:

Childhood: With each chapter we become increasingly more aware of the world around us during our years of biological growth;

Adolescence: We determine how to effectively exist independent of our guardian(s);

Young Adult: We develop a biological and emotional desire to give love and be intimately loved by another human being;

Adult: We seek a vocation to provide us with the basic necessities of human existence;

Advanced Adult Years: We produce and nurture offspring to perpetuate our legacy of having once existed here on Earth;

Golden Years of Life: With age comes the increased probability of disease and physical deterioration, thus, we retire to rest and review each chapter of the life story we have created.

These six basic sections of our book of life have multiple chapters based on salient events that unexpectedly alter intended life outcomes. Unlike book chapters, these sections of life have no hard cutoffs or boundaries. Time and biological forces do not permit us to rearrange them in a desired sequence. Some teenagers may think that, based on their vast life experience, they have more knowledge of life's secrets than those individuals who have lived the later chapters of life. What they do possess is the advantage of freedom from the dogmatic self-inflicted social constraints that many adults have written into their lives as boundaries.

At any moment, fate can intervene to create a new life chapter. Fate has both its perils and its virtues. During our formative years of life, we begin to discover how the world around us is supposed to work. Because childhood is the fertile soil where our moral, spiritual, and ethical values are rooted, certain disruptions of fate during this section of our life can linger for a lifetime. If you have been reading this book in chapter sequence you may have noticed how most of the introductions to each quote began with a story from my formative years of development. Our childhood/adolescence is the substrate from which we grow our adult emotional health and stability. Childhood/adolescence can also be the unfortunate, dark cauldron from which our life's demons and dragons (abuse, addiction, prejudice, greed, disregard for life, etc.) arise to haunt us throughout our adult years.

During each era of life, a new chapter develops, and fate creates an unexpected plot twist. So, let's take a moment for a final pop quiz on life expectations:

Are you in the vocation you expected to be doing when you left high school?

How many of your friends have changed their vocation since college?

How many times have you said to yourself, "That would never happen to me," only to have fate prove that you do not have total control over how your life chapters will be edited?

Just because you have always done everything according to the accepted social/cultural norms, has your life always (at least 80 percent of the time) gone the way you planned it?

When asked, many extremely successful people living out their golden years admit a random sequence of unanticipated events was the nidus of their ultimate success. While they were developing their carefully scripted chapters of life, fate intervened with failures, misfortune, death, disease, misadventures, or missed opportunities. Fate also revealed opportunities for success, good fortune, the birth of new ideas, miraculous cures, joyfully unexpected adventures, new companionships, and infinite opportunities. In order to get to the latter chapters of joy we often have to struggle through the initial chapters of misery.

Each of these twists of fate punctuate a necessary section of life. They are unavoidable and should be an expected variable of life. Instead of cursing your fate in life, celebrate it as an opportunity to gain another foothold in climbing toward unimagined life summits.

The virtue of fate will come disguised in many ways. It may arrive as a poolside bully or a soulmate you unexpectedly meet while on a walk in the park. It may arrive on your journey to find truth and wisdom during a contentious debate. A virtuous twist of fate could come to you while trapped in the darkness of an unanticipated life situation; or in a fictional story conjured up in a dream. It could also arrive with the death or loss of someone you loved dearly. Fate has its virtue, prompting you to write your next life chapter when the time is correct to do so. Review your life chapters and learn from each. When adversity arrives, prayerfully wait in silence for fate and circumstance to grant you a special delivery message of salvation from the edge of nowhere.

The louder I give love, the more I will experience the immeasurable reverberating joy of a life well lived.

We write our book of life; but God has ownership of the entire library.

Epilogue

During the introduction of this book I stated, "My unscientific observation is that most, if not all, great accomplishments occur through a sequence of random, yet unique, life experiences that become linked with personal life opportunities we are exposed to in our daily lives. Based on input achieved through our biological sensory receptors that allow us to see, touch, smell, hear, taste, and experience our environment, we collect critical information that allows us to be better or worse human beings than we were the day before."

After completing the initial draft of the final chapter of the book, I was flying home from a conference. It was 11:54 p.m. on a Sunday. I was exhausted but happy to be coming home. The aircraft captain announced we were about to make our final approach for landing in Dayton, Ohio. A muffled announcement over the intercom asked the flight attendants to please be seated.

From my seat in 13A, I looked out of the window as the aircraft glided above what seemed like an endless ocean of white fluffy clouds brightened by the moon's glow. The cabin was illuminated now by the sequence of the red and orange no smoking and seat belt signs overhead. I could hear the faint mechanical hum of the jet's engine, situated just beneath the wing outside my window, efficiently siphoning air through its turbines.

Out in the distance I could see the blinking lights of two other airplanes also situated above an ocean of clouds. I presumed they were also preparing to land. For a brief moment, my thoughts turned to the people on the two planes floating out there in the distance. I wondered if someone was sitting on one of those planes looking out their window seeing the plane I was on, thinking about the passengers on my plane as I was thinking about the passengers on theirs. Although I understand the physics of lift, drag, and the aerodynamics the aircraft uses to allow it to defy gravity, I still marvel at the fact that I am safely sitting in a metal cylinder flying above the clouds. In that moment, it took me back to the first time I recalled sitting on the concrete steps of my back porch on Williams Street looking up at the night sky as a plane flew over. Even then I wondered what made planes fly like birds, without benefit of flapping wings. I recall my failed attempts at trying to fly out of the swings at Riverview Park. I also wondered about the people up there flying in the plane. Who were they? Where were they going? Were they looking down at me on Earth? Could they even see me? If they could not see me, how could they care about me?

As I continued to look out of the window, the sea of stars embossed against the dark sky caught my attention. I pondered the space between the stars realizing that beyond my visual perception, trillions of suns and galaxies filled the gloomy black vacuum. Light years away, had the suns giving birth to the ancient lights I was witnessing been extinguished by time? Were there others out there in the space between stars looking in our direction pondering my existence? If they could not meet us, I wondered, how could they care about us?

If we want to speak a new language, the best method I know is to immerse ourselves in a culture that speaks that language. If we desire to find transformative solutions to social tribulations, we must immerse ourselves in the culture struggling with the problem we wish to solve.

If a visitor from a far-off world approached the beautiful blue planet we call Earth, would they see the same quiet little orb I was now about to land on? The visitor would not know the stories of our existence. The guest would not know the history of our evolution as human beings. The galactic tourist would certainly know nothing of the hopes and dreams existing in the souls of the residents inhabiting the earth. As I gazed out the plane's window, I realized the enormity of the human life chapters written each day. Those of the hundreds of souls on the two other planes floating above the clouds outside my window. Those of the fifty-three other souls sharing an experience with me on the aircraft I was traveling. Those of the inhabitants on the earth beneath the clouds. I thought about them all in that instant. Had they transitioned from awareness to wisdom by mastering the art of noticing the unnoticed treasures of life hidden in these stories of a shared human existence? For one brief moment God granted me the power to care about them all, even the ones whose book of stories had concluded or been forgotten like the light of a distant burned-out star.

As our plane quietly drifted down into the ocean of clouds, I thought once again of the visitors I imagined as a child sitting on my backyard steps. I imagined them journeying from their world somewhere from the edge of nowhere. Like me, they were about to land on the lonely little planet three worlds away from its life-sustaining star. The visitors' arrival was a voyage of verification. They had come to authenticate that the inhabitants had received their distant communications; and if so, verify they had used their ember messages of awareness to launch Earth's inhabitants toward a destination of genuine wisdom — sent to them from the edge of nowhere.

⋅⊰═⊱⋅

"Seek the beauty in everything and everyone."

Acknowledgments

To Mommy
My sincere thanks to my children, for giving me the little brown book as a gift with their hand written inscription. It eventually inspired me to compose this book.

Thank you to Patty, who read the initial chapters and encouraged me to write more.

Thank you to Ann for editing my manuscript and suggesting I share the finished product with the world.

Thank you to all the angels in my life who consistently pointed towards a life filled with joyful purpose;

And a very special thanks to the Creator of each sentinel angel who were ever present in my life to whisper truth and wisdom to my spirit - from the edge of nowhere.

Afterword

The final chapter written for this book is entitled: "Fate has it virtue." The *Quotes From the Edge of Nowhere* were heard and written long before the year 2020. However, the messages shared in this book have not been diluted by the passage of time. Our world as we once understood it was turned upside down by the arrival of an invisible viral pandemic that unearthed very visible social inequalities. The final chapter for humanity has not been written.

Our spirits and our bodies cannot rest easy in a land where injustice is given justification. May we strive instead to emerge from this shared planetary experience as more wise, just, and compassionate human beings.

G. LeRoy, M.D.

CPSIA information can be obtained
at www.ICGtesting.com
Printed in the USA
BVHW040816030321
601585BV00003B/15